MEMOIR

OF

OLD ELIZABETH,

A

COLOURED WOMAN

and other testimonies

"There is neither Jew nor Greek, there is neither bond nor free, there is neither male nor female, for ye are all one in Christ Jesus."

GAL. iii. 25.

Cover picture: Sojourner Truth

ISBN: 9781849027212

© 2010 Benediction Classics, Oxford.

"By our sufferings, since ye brought us
To the man-degrading mart,–
All sustain'd by patience, taught us
Only by a broken heart,–
Deem our nation brutes no longer,
Till some reason ye shall find
Worthier of regard, and stronger
Than the colour of our kind."

William Cowper

Contents

Memoir of Old Elizabeth, a coloured woman

In the following Narrative of "OLD ELIZABETH," which was taken mainly from her own lips in her 97th year, her simple language has been adhered to as strictly as was consistent with perspicuity and propriety.

I was born in Maryland in the year 1766. My parents were slaves. Both my father and mother were religious people, and belonged to the Methodist Society. It was my father's practice to read in the Bible aloud to his children every Sabbath morning. At these seasons, when I was but five years old, I often felt the overshadowing of the Lord's Spirit, without at all understanding what it meant; and these incomes and influences continued to attend me until I was eleven years old, particularly when I was alone, by which I was preserved from doing anything that I thought was wrong.

In the eleventh year of my age, my master sent me to another farm, several miles from my parents, brothers, and sisters, which was a great trouble to me. At last I grew so lonely and sad I thought I should die, if I did not see my mother. I asked the overseer if I might go, but being positively denied, I concluded to go without his knowledge. When I reached home my mother was away. I set off and walked twenty miles before I found her. I staid with her for several days, and we returned together. Next day I was sent back to my new place, which renewed my sorrow. At parting, my mother told me that I had "nobody in the wide world to look to but God." These words fell upon my heart with ponderous weight, and seemed to add to my grief. I went back repeating as I went, "none but God in the wide world." On reaching the farm, I found the overseer was displeased at me for going without his liberty. He tied me with a rope, and gave me some stripes of which I carried the marks for weeks.

After this time, finding as my mother said, I had none in the world to look to but God, I betook myself to prayer, and in every lonely place I found an altar. I mourned sore like a dove and chattered forth my sorrow, moaning in the corners of the field, and under the fences.

I continued in this state for about six months, feeling as though my head were waters, and I could do nothing but weep. I lost my appetite, and not being able to take enough food to sustain nature, I became so weak I had but little strength to work; still I was required to do all my duty. One evening, after the duties of the day were ended, I thought I could not live over the night, so threw myself on a bench, expecting to die, and without being prepared to meet my Maker; and my spirit cried within me, must I die in this state, and be banished from Thy presence forever? I own I am a sinner in Thy sight, and not fit to live where thou art. Still it was my fervent desire that the Lord would pardon me. Just at this season, I saw with my spiritual eye, an awful gulf of misery. As I thought I was about to plunge into it, I heard a voice saying, "rise up and pray," which strengthened me. I fell on my knees and prayed the best I could the Lord's prayer. Knowing no more to say, I halted, but continued on my knees. My spirit was then *taught* to pray, "Lord, have mercy on me—Christ save me." Immediately there appeared a director, clothed in white raiment. I thought he took me by the hand and said, "come with me." He led me down a long journey to a fiery gulf, and left me standing upon the brink of this awful pit. I began to scream for mercy, thinking I was about to be plunged to the belly of hell, and believed I should sink to endless ruin. Although I prayed and wrestled with all my might, it seemed in vain. Still, I felt all the while that I was sustained by some invisible power. At this solemn moment, I thought I saw a hand from which hung, as it were, a silver hair, and a voice told me that all the hope I had of being saved was no more than a hair; still, pray, and it will be sufficient. I then renewed my struggle, crying for mercy and salvation, until I found that every cry raised me higher and higher, and my head was quite above the fiery pillars. Then I thought I was permitted to look straight forward, and saw the Saviour standing with His hand stretched out to receive me. An indescribably glorious light was *in* Him, and He said, "peace, peace, come unto me." At this moment I felt that my sins were forgiven me, and the time of my deliverance was at hand. I sprang forward and fell at his feet, giving Him all the thanks and highest praises, crying, Thou hast redeemed me—Thou hast redeemed me to thyself. I felt filled with light and love. At this moment I thought my former guide took me again by the hand and led me upward, till I came to the celestial world and to heaven's door, which I saw was open, and while I stood there, a power surrounded me which drew me in, and I saw millions of glorified spirits in white robes. After I had this view, I thought I heard a voice saying, "Art thou willing to be saved?" I said, Yes Lord. Again I was asked, "Art thou willing to be saved in my way?" I stood speechless until he asked me again, "Art thou willing to be saved in my way?" Then I heard a whispering voice say, "If thou art not saved in the Lord's way, thou canst not be saved at all;" at which I exclaimed, "Yes Lord, in thy own way." Immediately a light fell upon my head, and I was filled with light, and I was shown the world lying in wickedness, and was told I must go there, and call the people to repentance, for the day of the Lord was at hand; and this message was as a heavy yoke upon me, so that I wept bitterly at the thought of what I should have to pass through. While I wept, I heard a voice say, "weep not, some will laugh at thee, some will scoff at thee, and the dogs will bark at thee, but while thou doest my will, I will be with thee to the ends of the earth."

I was at this time not yet thirteen years old. The next day, when I had come to myself, I felt like a new creature in Christ, and all my desire was to see the Saviour.

I lived in a place where there was no preaching, and no religious instruction; but every day I went out amongst the hay-stacks, where the presence of the Lord overshadowed me, and I was filled with sweetness and joy, and was as a vessel filled with holy oil. In this way I continued for about a year; many times while my hands were at my work, my spirit was carried away to spiritual things. One day as I was going to my old place behind the hay-stacks to pray, I was assailed with this language, "Are you going there to weep and pray? what a fool! there are older professors than you are, and they do not take that way to get to heaven; people whose sins are forgiven ought to be joyful and lively, and not be struggling and praying." With this I halted and concluded I would not go, but do as other professors did, and so went off to play; but at this moment the light that was in me became darkened, and the peace and joy that I once had, departed from me.

About this time I was moved back to the farm where my mother lived, and then sold to a stranger. Here I had deep sorrows and plungings, not having experienced a return of that sweet evidence and light with which I had been favoured formerly; but by watching unto prayer, and wrestling mightily with the Lord, my peace gradually returned, and with it a great exercise and weight upon my heart for the salvation of my fellow-creatures; and I was often carried to distant lands and shown places where I should have to travel and deliver the Lord's message. Years afterwards, I found myself visiting those towns and countries that I had seen in the light as I sat at home at my sewing,—places of which I had never heard.

Some years from this time I was sold to a Presbyterian for a term of years, as he did not think it right to hold slaves for life. Having served him faithfully my time out, he gave me my liberty, which was about the thirtieth year of my age.

As I now lived in a neighborhood where I could attend religious meetings, occasionally I felt moved to speak a few words therein; but I shrank from it—so great was the cross to my nature.

I did not speak much till I had reached my forty-second year, when it was revealed to me that the message which had been given to me I had not yet delivered, and the time had come. As I could read but little, I questioned within myself how it would be possible for me to deliver the message, when I did not understand the Scriptures. Whereupon I was moved to open a Bible that was near me, which I did, and my eyes fell upon this passage, "Gird up thy loins now like a man, and answer thou me. Obey God rather than man," &c. Here I fell into a great exercise of spirit, and was plunged very low. I went from one religious professor to another, enquiring of them what ailed me; but of all these I could find none who could throw any light upon such impressions. They all told me there was nothing in Scripture that would sanction such exercises. It was hard for men to travel, and what would women do? These things greatly discouraged me, and shut up my way, and caused me to resist the Spirit. After going to all that were accounted pious, and receiving no help, I returned to the Lord, feeling that I was nothing, and knew nothing, and wrestled and prayed to the Lord that He would fully reveal His will, and make the way plain.

Whilst I thus struggled, there seemed a light from heaven to fall upon me, which banished all my desponding fears, and I was enabled to form a new resolution to go on to prison and to death, if it might be my portion: and the Lord showed me that it was His will I should be resigned to die any death that might be my lot, in carrying his message, and be entirely crucified to the world, and sacrifice *all* to His glory that was then in my possession, which His witnesses, the holy Apostles, had done before me. It was then revealed to me that the Lord had given me the evidence of a clean heart, in which I could rejoice day and night, and I walked and talked with God, and my soul was illuminated with heavenly light, and I knew nothing but Jesus Christ, and him crucified.

One day, after these things, while I was at my work, the Spirit directed me to go to a poor widow, and ask her if I might have a meeting at her house, which was situated in one of the lowest and worst streets in Baltimore. With great joy she gave notice, and at the time appointed I appeared there among a few coloured sisters. When they had all prayed, they called upon me to close the meeting, and I felt an impression that I must say a few words; and while I was speaking, the house seemed filled with light; and when I was about to close the meeting, and was kneeling, a man came in and stood till I arose. It proved to be a watchman. The sisters became so frightened, they all went away except the one who lived in the house, and an old woman; they both appeared to be much frightened, fearing they should receive some personal injury, or be put out of the house. A feeling of weakness came over me for a short time, but I soon grew warm and courageous in the Spirit. The man then said to me, "I was sent here to break up your meeting. Complaint has been made to me that the people round here cannot sleep for the racket." I replied, "a good racket is better than a bad racket. How do they rest when the ungodly are dancing and fiddling till midnight? Why are not they molested by the watchmen? and why should we be for praising God, our Maker? Are we worthy of greater punishment for praying to Him? and are we to be prohibited from doing so, that sinners may remain slumbering in their sins?" While speaking these few words I grew warm with *heavenly* zeal, and laid my hand upon him and addressed him with gospel truth, "how do sinners sleep in hell, after slumbering in their sins here, and crying, 'let me rest, let me rest,' while sporting on the very brink of hell? Is the cause of God to be destroyed for this purpose?" Speaking several words more to this amount, he turned pale and trembled, and begged my pardon, acknowledging that it was not his wish to interrupt us, and that he would never disturb a religious assembly again. He then took leave of me in a comely manner and wished us success. After he was gone, I turned to the old sisters who by this time were quite cheered up. You see, said I, if the sisters had not fled, what a victory we might have had on the Lord's side; for the man seemed ready to give up under conviction. If it had not been for their cowardice, we might have all bowed in prayer, and a shout of victory had been heard amongst us.

Our meeting gave great offence, and we were forbid holding any more assemblies. Even the elders of our meeting joined with the wicked people, and said such meetings must be stopped, and that woman quieted. But I was not afraid of any of them, and continued to go, and burnt with a zeal not my own. The old sisters were zealous sometimes, and at other times would sink under the cross. Thus they grew cold, at which I was much grieved. I proposed to them to ask the elders to send a brother, which was concluded upon.

We went on for several years, and the Lord was with us with great power it proved, to the conversion of many souls, and we continued to grow stronger.

I felt at times that I must exercise in the ministry, but when I rose upon my feet I felt ashamed, and so I went under a cloud for some time, and endeavoured to keep silence; but I could not quench the Spirit. I was rejected by the elders and rulers, as Christ was rejected by the Jews before me, and while others were excused in crimes of the darkest dye, I was hunted down in every place where I appointed a meeting. Wading through many sorrows, I thought at times I might as well be banished from this life, as to feel the Almighty drawing me one way, and man another; so that I was tempted to cast myself into the dock. But contemplating the length of eternity, and how long my sufferings would be in that unchangeable world, compared with this, if I endured a little longer, the Lord was pleased to deliver me from this gloomy, melancholy state in his own time; though while this temptation lasted I roved up and down, and talked and prayed.

I often felt that I was unfit to assemble with the congregation with whom I had gathered, and had sometimes been made to rejoice in the Lord. I felt that I was despised on account of this gracious calling, and was looked upon as a speckled bird by the ministers to whom I looked for instruction, and to whom I resorted every opportunity for the same; but when I would converse with them, some would cry out,

"You are an enthusiast;" and others said, "the Discipline did not allow of any such division of the work;" until I began to think I surely must be wrong. Under this reflection, I had another gloomy cloud to struggle through; but after awhile I felt much moved upon by the Spirit of the Lord, and meeting with an aged sister, I found upon conversing with her that she could sympathize with me in this spiritual work. She was the first one I had met with, who could fully understand my exercises. She offered to open her house for a meeting, and run the risk of all the church would do to her for it. Many were afraid to open their houses in this way, lest they should be turned out of the church.

I persevered, notwithstanding the opposition of those who were looked upon as higher and wiser. The meeting was appointed, and but few came. I felt much backwardness, and as though I could not pray, but a pressure upon me to arise and express myself by way of exhortation. After hesitating for some time whether I would take up the cross or no, I arose, and after expressing a few words, the Spirit came upon me with life, and a victory was gained over the power of darkness, and we could rejoice together in His love.

As for myself, I was so full I hardly knew whether I was in the body, or out of the body—so great was my joy for the victory on the Lord's side. But the persecution against me increased, and a complaint was carried forward, as was done formerly against Daniel, the servant of God, and the elders came out with indignation for my holding meetings contrary to discipline—being a woman.

Thus we see when the heart is not inspired, and the inward eye enlightened by the Spirit, we are incapable of discerning the mystery of God in these things. Individuals creep into the church that are unregenerate, and after they have been there awhile, they fancy that they have got the grace of God, while they are destitute of it. They may have a degree of light in their heads, but evil in their hearts; which makes them think they are qualified to be judges of the ministry, and their conceit makes them very busy in matters of religion, judging of the revelations that are given to others, while they have received none themselves. Being thus mistaken, they are calculated to make a great deal of confusion in the church, and clog the true ministry.

These are they who eat their own bread, and wear their own apparel, having the form of godliness, but are destitute of the power.

Again I felt encouraged to attend another and another appointment. At one of these meetings, some of the class-leaders were present, who were constrained to cry out, "Surely the Lord has *revealed* these things to her" and asked one another if they ever heard the like? I look upon man as a very selfish being, when placed in a religious office, to presume to resist the work of the Almighty; because He does not work by man's authority. I did not faint under discouragement, but pressed on.

Under the contemplation of these things, I slept but little, being much engaged in receiving the revelations of the Divine will concerning this work, and the mysterious call thereto.

I felt very unworthy and small, notwithstanding the Lord had shown himself with great power, insomuch that conjecturers and critics were constrained to join in praise to his great name; for truly, we had times of refreshing from the presence of the Lord. At one of the meetings, a vast number of the white inhabitants of the place, and many coloured people, attended—many no doubt from curiosity to hear what the old coloured woman had to say. One, a great scripturian, fixed himself behind the door with pen and ink, in order to take down the discourse in short-hand; but the Almighty Being anointed me with such a portion of his Spirit, that he cast away his paper and pen, and heard the discourse with patience, and was much affected, for the Lord wrought powerfully on his heart. After meeting, he came forward and offered me his hand with solemnity on his countenance, and handed me something to pay for my conveyance home.

I returned, much strengthened by the Lord's power, to go on to the fulfilment of His work, although I was again pressed by the authorities of the church to which I belonged, for imprudency; and so much condemned, that I was sorely tempted by the enemy to turn aside into the wilderness. I was so embarrassed and encompassed, I wondered within myself whether all that were called to be mouth piece for the Lord, suffered such deep wadings as I experienced.

I now found I had to travel still more extensively in the work of the ministry, and I applied to the Lord for direction. I was often *invited* to go hither and thither, but felt that I must wait for the dictates of His Spirit.

At a meeting which I held in Maryland, I was led to speak from the passage, "Woe to the rebellious city," &c. After the meeting, the people came where I was, to take me before the squire; but the Lord delivered me from their hands.

I also held meetings in Virginia. The people there would not believe that a coloured woman could preach. And moreover, as she had no learning, they strove to imprison me because I spoke against slavery: and being brought up, they asked by what authority I spake? and if I had been ordained? I answered, not by the commission of men's hands: if the Lord had ordained me, I needed nothing better.

As I travelled along through the land, I was led at different times to converse with white men who were by profession ministers of the gospel. Many of them, up and down, confessed they did not believe in revelation, which gave me to see that men were sent forth as ministers without Christ's authority. In a conversation with one of these, he said, "You think you have these things by revelation, but there has been no such thing as revelation since Christ's ascension." I asked him where the apostle John got his revelation while he was in the Isle of Patmos. With this, he rose up and left me, and I said in my spirit, get thee behind me Satan.

I visited many remote places, where there were no meeting houses, and held many glorious meetings, for the Lord poured out his Spirit in sweet effusions. I also travelled in Canada, and visited several settlements of coloured people, and felt an open door amongst them.

I may here remark, that while journeying through the different states of the Union, I met with many of the Quaker Friends, and visited them in their families. I received much kindness and sympathy, and no opposition from them, in the prosecution of my labours.

On one occasion, in a thinly settled part of the country, seeing a Friend's meeting house open, I went in; at the same time a Friend and his little daughter followed me. We three composed the meeting. As we sat there in silence, I felt a remarkable overshadowing of the Divine presence, as much so as I ever experienced any where. Toward the close, a few words seemed to be given me, which I expressed, and left the place greatly refreshed in Spirit. From thence I went to Michigan, where I found a wide field of labour amongst my own colour.

Here I remained four years. I established a school for coloured orphans, having always felt the great importance of the religious and
moral *agri*culture of children, and the great need of it, especially
amongst the coloured people. Having white teachers, I met with much
encouragement.

My eighty-seventh year had now arrived, when suffering from
disease, and feeling released from travelling further in my good Master's cause, I came on to Philadelphia, where I have remained until this
time, which brings me to my ninety-seventh year. When I went forth,
it was without purse or scrip,—and I have come through great tribula-
tion and temptation—not by any might of my own, for I feel that I am
but as dust and ashes before my almighty Helper, who has, according
to His promise, been with me and sustained me through all, and gives
me now firm faith that he will be with me to the end, and, in his own
good time, receive me into His everlasting rest.

Lucinda Davis
Tulsa, Oklahoma

What yo' gwine do when de meat give out?
What yo' gwine do when da meat give out?
Set in de corner wid my lips pooched out!
Lawsy!

What yo' gwine do when de meat come in?
What yo' gwine do when da meat come in?
Set in de corner wid a greasy chin!
Lawsy!

Dat's about de only little nigger song I know, less'n it be de one about:

"Great big nigger, laying 'hind de log—
Finger on de trigger and eye on the hawg!
Click go de trigger and bang go de gun!
Here come de owner and de buck nigger run!"

And I think I learn both of dem long after I been grown, 'cause I belong to a full-blood Creek Indian and I didn't know nothing but Creek talk long after de Civil War. My mistress was part white and knowed English talk, but she never did talk it because none of de people talked it. I heard it sometime, but it sound like whole lot of wild shoat in de cedar brake scared at something when I do hear it. Dat was when I was little girl in time of de War.

I don't know where I been born. Nobody never did tell me. But my mammy and pappy git me after de War and I know den whose child I is. De men at de Creek Agency help 'em git me, I reckon, maybe.

First thing I remember is when I was a little girl, and I belong to old Tuskaya-hiniha. He was big man in de Upper Creek, and we have a purty good size farm, jest a little bit to de north of de wagon depot houses on de old road at Honey Springs. Dat place was about twenty-five mile south of Fort Gibson, but I don't know nothing about whar de fort is when I was a little girl at dat time. I know de Elk River 'bout two mile north of whar we live, 'cause I been there many de time.

I don't know if old Master have a white name. Lots de Upper Creek didn't have no white name. Maybe he have another Indian name, too, because Tuskayahiniha mean "head man warrior" in Creek, but dat what everybody call him and dat what de family call him too.

My Mistress' name was Nancy, and she was a Lott before she marry old man Tuskaya-hiniha. Her pappy name was Lott and he was purty near white. Maybe so all white. Dey have two chillun, I think, but only one stayed on de place. She was name Luwina, and her hus-bana was dead. His name was Walker, and Luwina bring Mr. Walker's little sister, Nancy, to live at de place too.

Luwina had a little baby boy and dat de reason old Master buy me, to look after de little baby boy. He didn't have no name cause he wasn't big enough when I was with dem, but he git a name later on, I reckon. We all call him "Istidji." Dat mean "little man."

When I first remember, before de War, old Master had 'bout as many slave as I got fingers, I reckon. I can think dem off on my fingers like dis, but I can't recollect de names.

Dey call all de slaves "Istilusti." Dat mean "black man."

Old man Tuskaya-hiniha was near 'bout blind before de War, and 'bout time of de War he go plumb blind and have to set on de long seat under de bresh shelter of de house all de time. Sometime I lead him around de yard a little, but not very much. Dat about de time all de slave begin to slip out and run off.

My own pappy was name Stephany. I think he take dat name 'cause when he little his mammy call him "Istifani." Dat mean a skeleton, and he was a skinny man. He belong to de Grayson family and I think his master name George, but I don't know. Dey big people in de Creek, and with de white folks too. My mammy name was Serena and she belong to some of de Gouge family. Dey was big people in de Upper Creek, and one de biggest men of the Gouge was name Hopoethleyoholo for his Creek name. He was a big man and went to de North in de War and died up in Kansas, I think. Dey say when he was a littla boy he was called Hopoethli, which mean "good little boy", and when he git grown he make big speeches and dey stick on de "yoholo." Dat mean "loud whooper."

Dat de way de Creek made de name for young boys when I was a little girl. When de boy git old enough de big men in de town give him a name, and sometime later on when he git to going round wid de grown men dey stick on some more name. If he a good talker dey sometime stick on "yoholo", and iffen he make lots of jokes dey call him "Hadjo." If he is a good leader dey call him "Imala" and if he kind of mean dey sometime call him "fixigo."

My mammy and pappy belong to two masters, but dey live together on a place. Dat de way de Creek slaves do lots of times. Dey work patches and give de masters most all dey make, but dey have some for demselves. Dey didn't have to stay on de master's place and work like I hear de slave of de white people and de Cherokee and Choctaw people say dey had to.

Maybe my pappy and mammy run off and git free, or maybeso dey buy demselves out, but anyway dey move away some time and my mammy's master sell me to old man Tuskaya-hiniha when I was jest a little gal. All I have to do is stay at de house and mind de baby.

Master had a good log house and a bresh shelter out in front like all de houses had. Like a gallery, only it had de dirt for de flo' and bresh for de roof. Dey cook everything out in de yard in big pots, and dey eat out in de yard too.

Dat was sho' good stuff to eat, and it make you fat too! Roast de green corn on de ears in de ashes, and scrape off some and fry it! Grind de dry corn or pound it up and make ash cake. Den bile de greens--all kinds of greens from out in de woods--and chip up de pork and deer meat, or de wild turkey meat; maybe all of dem, in de big pot at de same time! Fish too, and de big turtle dat lay out on de bank!

Dey always have a pot full of sofki settin right inside de house, and anybody eat when dey feel hungry. Anybody come on a visit, always give 'em some of de sofki. Ef dey don't take none de old man git mad, too!

When you make de sofki you pound up the corn real fine, den pour in de water and dreen it off to git all de little skin from off'n de grain. Den you let de grits soak and den bile it and let it stand. Sometime you put in some pounded hickory nut meats. Dat make it real good.

I don't know whar old Master git de cloth for de clothes, less'n he buy it. Befo' I can remember I think he had some slaves dat weave de cloth, but when I was dar he git it at de wagon depot at Honey Springs, I think. He go dar all de time to sell his corn, and he raise lots of corn, too.

Dat place was on de big road, what we called de road to Texas, but it go all de way up to de North, too. De traders stop at Honey Springs and old Master trade corn for what he want. He git some purty checkedy cloth one time, and everybody git a dress or a shirt made off'n it. I have dat dress 'till I git too big for it.

Everybody dress up fine when dey is a funeral. Dey take me along to mind de baby at two-three funerals, but I don't know who it is dat die. De Creek sho' take on when somebody die!

Long in de night you wake up and hear a gun go off, way off yonder somewhar. Den it go again, and den again, jest as fast as dey can ram de load in. Dat mean somebody dead. When somebody die de men go out in de yard and let de people know dat way. Den dey jest go back in de house and let de fire go out, and don't even tech de dead person till somebody git dar what has de right to tech de dead.

When somebody had sick dey build a fire in de house, even in de summer, and don't let it die down till dat person git well or die. When dey die dey let de fire go out.

In de morning everybody dress up fine and go to de house whar de dead is and stand around in de yard outside de house and don't go in. Pretty soon along come somebody what got a right to tech and handle de dead and dey go in. I don't know what give dem de right, but I think dey has to go through some kind of medicine to git de right, and I know dey has to drink de red root and purge good before dey tech de body. When dey git de body ready dey come out and all go to de graveyard, mostly de family graveyard, right on de place or at some of the kinfolkses.

When dey git to de grave somebody shoots a gun at de north, den de west, den de south, and den de east. Iffen dey had four guns dey used 'em.

Den dey put de body down in de grave and put some extra clothes in with it and some food and a cup of coffee, maybe. Den dey takes strips of elm bark and lays over de body till it all covered up, and den throw in de dirt.

When de last dirt throwed on, everybody must clap dey hands and smile, but you sho hadn't better step on any of de new dirt around de grave, because it bring sickness right along wid you back to your own house. Dat what dey said, anyways.

Jest soon as de grave filled up dey built a little shelter over it wid poles like a pig pen and kiver it over wid elm bark to keep de rain from soaking down in de new dirt.

Den everybody go back to de house and de family go in and scatter some kind of medicine 'round de place and build a new fire. Sometime dey feed everybody befo' dey all leave for home.

Every time dey have a funeral dey always a lot of de people say, "Didn't you hear de stinkini squalling in de night?" "I hear dat stikini all de night1" De "stikini" is de screech owl, and he suppose to tell when anybody going to die right soon. I hear lots of Creek people say dey hear de screech owl close to de house, and sho' nuff somebody in de family die soon.

When de big battle come at our place at Honey Springs dey jest git through having de green corn "busk." De green corn was just ripened enough to eat. It must of been along in July.

Dat busk was just a little busk. Dey wasn't enough men around to have a good one. But I seen lots of big ones. Ones whar dey had all de different kinds of "banga." Dey call all de dances some kind of banga. De chicken dance is de "Tolosabanga", and de "Istifanibanga" is de one whar dey make lak dey is skeletons and raw heads coming to git you.

De "Hadjobanga" is de crazy dance, and dat is a funny one. Dey all dance crazy and make up funny songs to go wid de dance. Everybody think up funny songs to sing and everybody whoop and laugh all de time.

But de worse one was de drunk dance. Dey jest dance ever whichaway, de men and de women together, and dey wrassle and hug and carry on awful! De good people don't dance dat one. Everybody sing about going to somebody elses house and sleeping wid dem, and shout, "We is all drunk and we don't know what we doing and we ain't doing wrong 'cause we is all drunk" and things like dat. Sometime de bad ones leave and go to de woods, too!

Dat kind of doing made de good people mad, and sometime dey have killings about it. When a man catch one his women--maybeso his wife or one of his daughters--been to de woods he catch her and beat her and cut off de rim of her ears! People think maybeso dat ain't so, but I know it is!

I was combing somebody's hair one time--I ain't going tell who-- and when I lift it up off'n her ears I nearly drap dead! Dar de rims cut right off'n 'em! But she was a married woman, and I think maybeso it happen when she was a young gal and got into it at one of dem drunk dances.

Dem Upper Creek took de marrying kind of light anyways. Iffen de younguns wanted to be man and wife and de old ones didn't care dey jest went ahead and dat was about all, 'cepting some presents maybe. But de Baptists changed dat a lot amongst de young ones.

I never forgit de day dat battle of de Civil War happen at Honey Springs! Old Master jest had de green corn all in, and us had been having a time getting it in, too. Jest de women was all dat was left, 'cause de men slaves had all slipped off and left out. My uncle Abe done got up a bunch and gone to de North wid dem to fight, but I didn't know den whar he went. He was in dat same battle, and after the War dey called him Abe Colonel. Most all de slaves 'round dat place done gone off a long time before dat wid dey masters when dey go wid old man Gouge and a man named McDaniel.

We had a big tree in de yard, and a grape vine swing in it for de little baby "Istidji", and I was swinging him real early in de morning befo' de sun up. De house set in a little patch of woods wid de field in de back, but all out on de north side was a little open space, like a kind of prairie. I was swinging de baby, and all at once I seen somebody riding dis way 'cross dat prairie--jest coming a-kiting and a-laying out flat out on his hoss. When he see de house he begin to give de war whoop, "Eya-a-a-a-he-ah!" When he git close to de house he holler to git out de way 'cause dey gwine to be a big fight, and old Master start rapping wid his cane and yelling to git some grub and blankets in de wagon right now!

We jest leave everything setting right whar it is, 'cepting putting out de fire and grabbing all de pots and kettles. Some de nigger women run to git de mules and de wagon and some start gitting meat and corn out of de place whar we done hid it to keep de scouters from finding it befo' now. All de time we gitting ready to travel we hear dat boy on dat horse going on down de big Texas road hollering "Eya-a-a-he-he-ah!"

Den jest as we starting to leave here come something across dat little prairie sho' nuff! We know dey is Indians de way dey is riding, and de way dey is all strung out. Dey had a flag, and it was all red and had a big criss-cross on it dat look lak a saw horse. De man carry it and rear back on it when de wind whip it, but it flap all 'round de horse's head and de horse pitch and rear lak he know something is going to happen, sho!

'Bout dat time it turn kind of dark and begin to rain a little, and we git out to de big road and de rain come down hard. It rain so hard for a little while dat we just have to stop de wagon and set dar, and den long come more soldiers dan I ever see befo'. Dey all white men, I think, and dey have on dat brown clothes dyed wid walnut and butternut, and old Master say dey de Confederate soldiers. Dey dragging some big guns on wheels and most de men slopping 'long in de rain on foot.

Den we hear de fighting up to de north 'long about what de river is, and de guns sound lak hosses loping 'cross a plank bridge way off somewhar. De head men starts hollering and some de hosses start rearing and de soldiers start trotting faster up de road. We can't git out on de road so we jest strike off through de prairie and make for a creek dat got high banks and a place on it we call Rocky Cliff.

We git in a big cave in dat cliff, and spend de whole day and dat night in dar, and listen to de battle going on. Dat place was about half-a-mile from de wagon depot at Honey Springs, and a little east of it. We can hear de guns going all day, and along in de evening here come de South side making for a getaway. Dey come riding and running by whar we is, and it don't make no difference how much he head men hollers at 'em dey can't make dat bunch slow up and stop.

After while here come de Yankees, right after 'em, and dey goes on into Honey Springs and pretty soon we see de blaze whar dey is burning depot and de houses.

De next morning we goes back to de house and find de soldiers ain't hurt nothing much. De hogs is whar dey is in de pen and de chickens come cackling 'round too. Dem soldiers going so fast dey didn't have no time to stop and take nothing, I reckon.

Den long come lots of de Yankee soldiers going back to the North, and dey looks purty wore out, but dey is laughing and joshing and going on.

Old Master pack up de wagon wid everything he can carry den, and we strike out down de big road to git out de way of any more war, is dey going to be any.

Dat old Texas road jest crowded wid wagons! Everybody doing de same thing we is, and de rains done made de road so muddy and de soldiers done tromp up de mud so bad dat de wagons git stuck all de time.

De people all moving along in bunches, and every little while one bunch of wagons come up wid another bunch all stuck in de mud, and dey put all de hosses and mules on together and pull em out, and den dey go on together awhile.

At night dey camp, and de women and what few niggers dey is have to git supper in de big pots, and de men so tired dey eat everything up from de women and de niggers, purty nigh.

After while we come to de Canadian town. Dat what old man Gouge been and took a whole lot de folks up north wid him, and de South soldiers got in dar ahead of us and took up all de houses to sleep in.

Dey was some of de white soldiers camped dar, and dey was singing at de camp. I couldn't understand what dey sing, and I asked a Creek man what dey say and he tell me dey sing, "I wish I was in Dixie, look away--look away."

I ask him whar dat is, and he laugh and talk to de soldiers and dey all laugh, and make me mad.

De next morning we leave dat town and git to de big river. De rain make de river rise, and I never see so much water! Jest look out dar and dar all dat water!

Dey got some boats we put de stuff on, and float de wagons and swim de mules and finally git across, but it look lak we gwine all drown.

Most de folks say dey going to Boggy Depot and around Fort Washita, but old Master strike off by hisself and go away down in de bottom somewhar to live.

I don't know whar it was, but dey been some kind of fighting all around dar, 'cause we camp in houses and cabins all de time and nobody live in any of 'em.

Look like de people all git away quick, 'cause all de stuff was in de houses, but you better scout up around de house before you go up to it. Liable to be some scouters already in it!

Dem Indian soldiers jest quit de army and lots went scouting in little bunches and took everything dey find. Iffen somebody try to stop dem dey git killed.

Sometime we find graves in de yard whar somebody jest been buried fresh, and one house had some dead people in it when old Mistress poke her head in it. We git away from dar, and no mistake!

By and by we find a little cabin and stop and stay all de time. I was de only slave by dat time. All de others done slip out and run off. We stay dar two year I reckon, 'cause we make two little crop of corn. For meat a man name Mr. Walker wid us jest went out in de woods and shoot de wild hogs. De woods was full of dem wild hogs, and lots of fish in de holes whar he could sicken 'em wid buck root and catch 'em wid his hands, all we wanted.

I don't know when de War quit off, and when I git free, but I stayed wid old man Tuskaya-hiniha long time after I was free, I reckon. I was jest a little girl, and he didn't know whar to send me to, anyways.

One day three men rid up and talk to de old man awhile in English talk. Den he called me and tell me to go wid dem to find my own family. He jest laugh and slap my behind and set me up on de hoss in front of one de men and dey take me off and leave my good checkedy dress at de house!

Before long we git to dat Canadian river again, and de men tie me on de hoss so I can't fall off. Dar was all dat water, and dey ain't no boat, and dey ain't no bridge, and we jest swim de hosses. I knowed sho' I was going to be gone dat time, but we git across.

When we came to de Creek Agency dar is my pappy and my mammy to claim me, and I live wid dem in de Verdigris bottom above Fort Gibson till I was grown and dey is both dead. Den I marries Anderson Davis at Gibson Station, and we git our allotments on de Verdigris east of Tulsa--kind of south too, close to de Broken Arrow town.

I knowed old man Jim McHenry at dat Broken Arrow town. He done some preaching and was a good old man, I think.

I knowed when dey started dat Wealaka school across de river from de Broken Arrow town. Dey name it for de Wilaki town, but dat town was way down in de Upper Creek country close to whar I lived when I was a girl.

I had lots of children, but only two is alive now. My boy Anderson got in a mess and went to dat McAlester prison, but he got to be a trusty and dey let him marry a good woman dat got lots of property dar, and dey living all right now.

When my old man die I come to live here wid Josephine, but I'se blind and can't see nothing and all de noises pesters me a lot in de town. And de children is all so ill mannered, too. Dey jest holler at you all de time! Dey don't mind you neither!

When I could see and had my own younguns I could jest set in de corner and tell 'em what to do, and iffen dey didn't do it right I could whack 'em on de head, 'cause dey was raised de old Creek way, and dey know de old folks know de best!

History of Mary Prince, a West Indian slave

I was born at Brackish-Pond, in Bermuda, on a farm belonging to Mr. Charles Myners. My mother was a household slave; and my father, whose name was Prince, was a sawyer belonging to Mr. Trimmingham, a ship-builder at Crow-Lane. When I was an infant, old Mr. Myners died, and there was a division of the slaves and other property among the family. I was bought along with my mother by old Captain Darrel, and given to his grandchild, little Miss Betsey Williams. Captain Williams, Mr. Darrel's son-in-law, was master of a vessel which traded to several places in America and the West Indies, and he was seldom at home long together.

Mrs. Williams was a kind-hearted good woman, and she treated all her slaves well. She had only one daughter, Miss Betsey, for whom I was purchased, and who was about my own age. I was made quite a pet of by Miss Betsey, and loved her very much. She used to lead me about by the hand, and call me her little nigger. This was the happiest period of my life; for I was too young to understand rightly my condition as a slave, and too thoughtless and full of spirits to look forward to the days of toil and sorrow.

My mother was a household slave in the same family. I was under her own care, and my little brothers and sisters were my playfellows and companions. My mother had several fine children after she came to Mrs. Williams,--three girls and two boys. The tasks given out to us children were light, and we used to play together with Miss Betsey, with as much freedom almost as if she had been our sister.

My master, however, was a very harsh, selfish man; and we always dreaded his return from sea. His wife was herself much afraid of him; and, during his stay at home, seldom dared to shew her usual kindness to the slaves. He often left her, in the most distressed circumstances, to reside in other female society, at some place in the West Indies of which I have forgot the name. My poor mistress bore his ill-treatment with great patience, and all her slaves loved and pitied her. I was truly attached to her, and, next to my own mother, loved her better than any creature in the world. My obedience to her commands was cheerfully

given: it sprung solely from the affection I felt for her, and not from fear of the power which the white people's law had given her over me.

I had scarcely reached my twelfth year when my mistress became too poor to keep so many of us at home; and she hired me out to Mrs. Pruden, a lady who lived about five miles off, in the adjoining parish, in a large house near the sea. I cried bitterly at parting with my dear mistress and Miss Betsey, and when I kissed my mother and brothers and sisters, I thought my young heart would break, it pained me so. But there was no help; I was forced to go. Good Mrs. Williams comforted me by saying that I should still be near the home I was about to quit, and might come over and see her and my kindred whenever I could obtain leave of absence from Mrs. Pruden. A few hours after this I was taken to a strange house, and found myself among strange people. This separation seemed a sore trial to me then; but oh! 'twas light, light to the trials I have since endured!--'twas nothing--nothing to be mentioned with them; but I was a child then, and it was according to my strength.

I knew that Mrs. Williams could no longer maintain me; that she was fain to part with me for my food and clothing; and I tried to submit myself to the change. My new mistress was a passionate woman; but yet she did not treat me very unkindly. I do not remember her striking me but once, and that was for going to see Mrs. Williams when I heard she was sick, and staying longer than she had given me leave to do. All my employment at this time was nursing a sweet baby, little Master Daniel; and I grew so fond of my nursling that it was my greatest delight to walk out with him by the sea-shore, accompanied by his brother and sister, Miss Fanny and Master James.--Dear Miss Fanny! She was a sweet, kind young lady, and so fond of me that she wished me to learn all that she knew herself; and her method of teaching me was as follows:--Directly she had said her lessons to her grandmamma, she used to come running to me, and make me repeat them one by one after her; and in a few months I was able not only to say my letters but to spell many small words. But this happy state was not to last long. Those days were too pleasant to last. My heart always softens when I think of them.

At this time Mrs. Williams died. I was told suddenly of her death, and my grief was so great that, forgetting I had the baby in my arms, I ran away directly to my poor mistress's house; but reached it only in time to see the corpse carried out. Oh, that was a day of sorrow,--a heavy day! All the slaves cried. My mother cried and lamented her sore; and I (foolish creature!) vainly entreated them to bring my dear mistress back to life. I knew nothing rightly about death then, and it seemed a hard thing to bear. When I thought about my mistress I felt as if the world was all gone wrong; and for many days and weeks I could think of nothing else. I returned to Mrs. Pruden's; but my sorrow was too great to be comforted, for my own dear mistress was always in my mind. Whether in the house or abroad, my thoughts were always talking to me about her.

I staid at Mrs. Pruden's about three months after this; I was then sent back to Mr. Williams to be sold. Oh, that was a sad sad time! I recollect the day well. Mrs. Pruden came to me and said, "Mary, you will have to go home directly; your master is going to be married, and he means to sell you and two of your sisters to raise money for the wedding." Hearing this I burst out a crying,--though I was then far from being sensible of the full weight of my misfortune, or of the misery that waited for me. Besides, I did not like to leave Mrs. Pruden, and the dear baby, who had grown very fond of me. For some time I could scarcely believe that Mrs. Pruden was in earnest, till I received orders for my immediate return.--Dear Miss Fanny! how she cried at parting with me, whilst I kissed and hugged the baby, thinking I should never see him again. I left Mrs. Pruden's, and walked home with a heart full of sorrow. The idea of being sold away from my mother and Miss Betsey was so frightful, that I dared not trust myself to think about it. We had been bought of Mr. Myners, as I have mentioned, by Miss Betsey's grandfather, and given to her, so that we were by right her property, and I never thought we should be separated or sold away from her.

When I reached the house, I went in directly to Miss Betsey. I found her in great distress; and she cried out as soon as she saw me, "Oh, Mary! my father is going to sell you all to raise money to marry that wicked woman. You are my slaves, and he has no right to sell you; but it is all to please her." She then told me that my mother was living with her father's sister at a house close by, and I went there to see her. It was a sorrowful meeting; and we lamented with a great and sore crying our unfortunate situation. "Here comes one of my poor picaninnies!" she said, the moment I came in, "one of the poor slave-brood who are to be sold to-morrow."

Oh dear! I cannot bear to think of that day,--it is too much.--It recalls the great grief that filled my heart, and the woeful thoughts that passed to and fro through my mind, whilst listening to the pitiful words of my poor mother, weeping for the loss of her children. I wish I could find words to tell you all I then felt and suffered. The great God above alone knows the thoughts of the poor slave's heart, and the bitter pains which follow such separations as these. All that we love taken away from us--Oh, it is sad, sad! and sore to be borne!--I got no sleep that night for thinking of the morrow; and dear Miss Betsey was scarcely less distressed. She could not bear to part with her old play-mates, and she cried sore and would not be pacified.

The black morning at length came; it came too soon for my poor mother and us. Whilst she was putting on us the new osnaburgs in which we were to be sold, she said, in a sorrowful voice, (I shall never forget it!) "See, I am shrouding my poor children; what a task for a mother!"--She then called Miss Betsey to take leave of us. "I am going to carry my little chickens to market," (these were her very words,) "take your last look of them; may be you will see them no more." "Oh, my poor slaves! my own slaves!" said dear Miss Betsey, "you belong to me; and it grieves my heart to part with you."--Miss Betsey kissed us all, and, when she left us, my mother called the rest of the slaves to bid us good bye. One of them, a woman named Moll,
came with her infant in her arms. "Ay!" said my mother, seeing her turn away and look at her child with the tears in her eyes, "your turn will come next." The slaves could say nothing to comfort us; they could only weep and lament with us. When I left my dear little brothers and the house in which I had been brought up, I thought my heart would burst.

Our mother, weeping as she went, called me away with the children Hannah and Dinah, and we took the road that led to Hamble Town, which we reached about four o'clock in the afternoon. We followed my mother to the market-place, where she placed us in row against a large house, with our backs to the wall and our arms folded across our breasts. I, as the eldest, stood first, Hannah next to me, then Dinah; and our mother stood beside, crying over us. My heart throbbed with grief and terror so violently, that I pressed my hands quite tightly across my breast, but I could not keep it still, and it continued to leap as though it would burst out of my body. But who cared for that? Did one of the many by-standers, who were looking at us so carelessly, think of the pain that wrung the hearts of the negro woman and her young ones? No, no! They were not all bad, I dare say, but slavery hardens white people's hearts towards the blacks; and many of them were not slow to make their remarks upon us aloud, without regard to our grief--though their light words fell like cayenne on the fresh wounds of our hearts. Oh those white people have small hearts who can only feel for themselves.

At length the vendue master, who was to offer, us for sale like sheep or cattle, arrived, and asked my mother which was the eldest. She said nothing, but pointed to me. He took me by the hand, and led me out into the middle of the street, and, turning me slowly round, exposed me to the view of those who attended the vendue. I was soon surrounded by strange men, who examined and handled me in the same manner that a butcher would a calf or a lamb he was about to purchase, and who talked about my shape and size in like words--as if I could no more understand their meaning than the dumb beasts. I was then put up to sale. The bidding commenced at a few pounds, and gradually rose to fifty-seven,[*] when I was knocked down to the highest bidder; and the people who stood by said that I had fetched a great sum for so young a slave.

I then saw my sisters led forth, and sold to different owners; so that we had not the sad satisfaction of being partners in bondage. When the sale was over, my mother hugged and kissed us, and mourned over us, begging of us to keep up a good heart, and do our

---

[*] Bermuda currency; about £38 sterling.

duty to our new masters. It was a sad parting; one went one way, one another, and our poor mammy went home with nothing. [†]

My new master was a Captain I--, who lived at Spanish Point. After parting with my mother and sisters, I followed him to his store, and he gave me into the charge of his son, a lad about my own age, Master Benjy, who took me to my new home. I did not know where I was going, or what my new master would do with me. My heart was quite broken with grief, and my thoughts went back continually to those from whom I had been so suddenly parted. "Oh, my mother! my mother!" I kept saying to myself, "Oh, my mammy and my sisters and my brothers, shall I never see you again!"

[†] Let the reader compare the above affecting account, taken down from the mouth of this negro woman, with the following description of a vendue of slaves at the Cape of Good Hope, published by me in 1826, from the letter of a friend,--and mark their similarity in several characteristic circumstances. The resemblance is easily accounted for: slavery wherever it prevails produces similar effects.--"Having heard that there was to be a sale of cattle, farm stock, &c. by auction, at a Veld-Cornet's in the vicinity, we halted our waggon one day for the purpose of procuring a fresh spann of oxen. Among the stock of the farm sold, was a female slave and her three children. The two eldest children were girls, the one about thirteen years of age, and the other about eleven; the youngest was a boy. The whole family were exhibited together, but they were sold separately, and to different purchasers. The farmers examined them as if they had been so many head of cattle. While the sale was going on, the mother and her children were exhibited on a table, that they might be seen by the company, which was very large. There could not have been a finer subject for an able painter than this unhappy group. The tears, the anxiety, the anguish of the mother, while she met the gaze of the multitude, eyed the different countenances of the bidders, or cast a heart-rending look upon the children; and the simplicity and touching sorrow of the young ones, while they clung to their distracted parent, wiping their eyes, and half concealing their faces,--contrasted with the marked insensibility and jocular countenances of the spectators and purchasers,--furnished a striking commentary on the miseries of slavery, and its debasing effects upon the hearts of its abettors. While the woman was in this distressed situation she was asked, 'Can you feed sheep?' Her reply was so indistinct that it escaped me; but it was probably in the negative, for her purchaser rejoined, in a loud and harsh voice, 'Then I will teach you with the sjamboc,' (a whip made of the rhinoceros' hide.) The mother and her three children were sold to three separate purchasers; and they were literally torn from each other."-- Ed.

Oh, the trials! the trials! they make the salt water come into my eyes when I think of the days in which I was afflicted--the times that are gone; when I mourned and grieved with a young heart for those whom I loved.

It was night when I reached my new home. The house was large, and built at the bottom of a very high hill; but I could not see much of it that night. I saw too much of it afterwards. The stones and the timber were the best things in it; they were not so hard as the hearts of the owners.‡

Before I entered the house, two slave women, hired from another owner, who were at work in the yard, spoke to me, and asked who I belonged to? I replied, "I am come to live here." "Poor child, poor child!" they both said; "you must keep a good heart, if you are to live here."--When I went in, I stood up crying in a corner. Mrs. I-- came and took off my hat, a little black silk hat Miss Pruden made for me, and said in a rough voice, "You are not come here to stand up in corners and cry, you are come here to work." She then put a child into my arms, and, tired as I was, I was forced instantly to
take up my old occupation of a nurse.--I could not bear to look at my mistress, her countenance was so stern. She was a stout tall woman with a very dark complexion, and her brows were always drawn together into a frown. I thought of the words of the two slave women when I saw Mrs. I--, and heard the harsh sound of her voice.

The person I took the most notice of that night was a French Black called Hetty, whom my master took in privateering from another vessel, and made his slave. She was the most active woman I ever saw, and she was tasked to her utmost. A few minutes after my arrival she came in from milking the cows, and put the sweet-potatoes on for supper. She then fetched home the sheep, and penned them in the fold; drove home the cattle, and staked them about the pond side;§ fed and rubbed down my master's horse, and gave the hog and the fed cow ** their suppers; prepared the beds, and undressed the children, and laid

---

‡ These strong expressions, and all of a similar character in this little narrative, are given verbatim as uttered by Mary Prince.-- Ed.

§ The cattle on a small plantation in Bermuda are, it seems, often thus staked or tethered, both night and day, in situations where grass abounds.

** A cow fed for slaughter.

28

them to sleep. I liked to look at her and watch all her doings, for hers was the only friendly face I had as yet seen, and I felt glad that she was there. She gave me my supper of potatoes and milk, and a blanket to sleep upon, which she spread for me in the passage before the door of Mrs. I--'s chamber.

I got a sad fright, that night. I was just going to sleep, when I heard a noise in my mistress's room; and she presently called out to inquire if some work was finished that she had ordered Hetty to do. "No, Ma'am, not yet," was Hetty's answer from below. On hearing this, my master started up from his bed, and just as he was, in his shirt, ran down stairs with a long cow-skin†† in his hand. I heard immediately after, the cracking of the thong, and the house rang to the shrieks of poor Hetty, who kept crying out, "Oh, Massa! Massa! me dead. Massa! have mercy upon me--don't kill me outright."--This was a sad beginning for me. I sat up upon my blanket, trembling with terror, like a frightened hound, and thinking that my turn would come next. At length the house became still, and I forgot for a little while all my sorrows by falling fast asleep.

The next morning my mistress set about instructing me in my tasks. She taught me to do all sorts of household work; to wash and bake, pick cotton and wool, and wash floors, and cook. And she taught me (how can I ever forget it!) more things than these; she caused me to know the exact difference between the smart of the rope, the cartwhip, and the cow-skin, when applied to my naked body by her own cruel hand. And there was scarcely any punishment more dreadful than the blows I received on my face and head from her hard heavy fist. She was a fearful woman, and a savage mistress to her slaves.

There were two little slave boys in the house, on whom she vented her bad temper in a special manner. One of these children was a mulatto, called Cyrus, who had been bought while an infant in his mother's arms; the other, Jack, was an African from the coast of Guinea, whom a sailor had given or sold to my master. Seldom a day passed without
these boys receiving the most severe treatment, and often for no fault at all. Both my master and mistress seemed to think that they had a right to ill-use them at their pleasure; and very often accompanied

---

†† (‡) A thong of hard twisted hide, known by this name in the West Indies.

their commands with blows, whether the children were behaving well or ill. I have seen their flesh ragged and raw with licks.--Lick--lick--they were never secure one moment from a blow, and their lives were passed in continual fear. My mistress was not contented with using the whip, but often pinched their cheeks and arms in the most cruel manner. My pity for these poor boys was soon transferred to myself; for I was licked, and flogged, and pinched by her pitiless fingers in the neck and arms, exactly as they were. To strip me naked--to hang me up by the wrists and lay my flesh open with the cow-skin, was an ordinary punishment for even a slight offence. My mistress often robbed me too of the hours that belong to sleep. She used to sit up very late, frequently even until morning; and I had then to stand at a bench and wash during the greater part of the night, or pick wool and cotton; and often I have dropped down overcome by sleep and fatigue, till roused from a state of stupor by the whip, and forced to start up to my tasks.

Poor Hetty, my fellow slave, was very kind to me, and I used to call her my Aunt; but she led a most miserable life, and her death was hastened (at least the slaves all believed and said so,) by the dreadful chastisement she received from my master during her pregnancy. It happened as follows. One of the cows had dragged the rope away from the stake to which Hetty had fastened it, and got loose. My master flew into a terrible passion, and ordered the poor creature to be stripped quite naked, notwithstanding her pregnancy, and to be tied up to a tree in the yard. He then flogged her as hard as he could lick, both with the whip and cow-skin, till she was all over streaming with blood. He rested, and then beat her again and again. Her shrieks were terrible. The consequence was that poor Hetty was brought to bed before her time, and was delivered after severe labour of a dead child. She appeared to recover after her confinement, so far that she was repeatedly flogged by both master and mistress afterwards; but her former strength never returned to her. Ere long her body and limbs swelled to a great size; and she lay on a mat in the kitchen, till the water burst out of her body and she died. All the slaves said that death was a good thing for poor Hetty; but I cried very much for her death. The manner of it filled me with horror. I could not bear to think about it; yet it was always present to my mind for many a day.

After Hetty died all her labours fell upon me, in addition to my own. I had now to milk eleven cows every morning before sunrise, sitting among the damp weeds; to take care of the cattle as well as the children; and to do the work of the house. There was no end to my toils--no end to my blows. I lay down at night and rose up in the morning in fear and sorrow; and often wished that like poor Hetty I could escape from this cruel bondage and be at rest in the grave. But the hand of that God whom then I knew not, was stretched over me; and I was mercifully preserved for better things. It was then, however, my heavy lot to weep, weep, weep, and that for years; to pass from one misery to another, and from one cruel master to a worse. But I must go on with the thread of my story.

One day a heavy squall of wind and rain came on suddenly, and my mistress sent me round the corner of the house to empty a large earthen jar. The jar was already cracked with an old deep crack that divided it in the middle, and in turning it upside down to empty it, it parted in my hand. I could not help the accident, but I was dreadfully frightened, looking forward to a severe punishment. I ran crying to my mistress, "O mistress, the jar has come in two." "You have broken it, have you?" she replied; "come directly here to me." I came trembling: she stripped and flogged me long and severely with the cow-skin; as long as she had strength to use the lash, for she did not give over till she was quite tired.--When my master came home at night, she told him of my fault; and oh, frightful! how he fell a swearing. After abusing me with every ill name he could think of, (too, too bad to speak in England,) and giving me several heavy blows with his hand, he said, "I shall come home to-morrow morning at twelve, on purpose to give you a round hundred." He kept his word--Oh sad for me! I cannot easily forget it. He tied me up upon a ladder, and gave me a hundred lashes with his own hand, and master Benjy stood by to count them for him. When he had licked me for some time he sat down to take breath; then after resting, he beat me again and again, until he was quite wearied, and so hot (for the weather was very sultry), that he sank back in his chair, almost like to faint. While my mistress went to bring him drink, there was a dreadful earthquake. Part of the roof fell down, and every thing in the house went--clatter, clatter, clatter. Oh I thought the end of all things near at hand; and I was so sore with the flogging, that I scarcely cared whether I lived or died. The earth was groaning and shaking; every thing tumbling about; and my mistress and the slaves were shrieking and crying out, "The earthquake! the earthquake!" It was an awful day for us all.

During the confusion I crawled away on my hands and knees, and laid myself down under the steps of the piazza, in front of the house. I was in a dreadful state--my body all blood and bruises, and I could not help moaning piteously. The other slaves, when they saw me, shook their heads and said, "Poor child! poor child!"--I lay there till the morning, careless of what might happen, for life was very weak in me, and I wished more than ever to die. But when we are very young, death always seems a great way off, and it would not come that night to me. The next morning I was forced by my master to rise and go about my usual work, though my body and limbs were so stiff and sore, that I could not move without the greatest pain.--Nevertheless, even after all this severe punishment, I never heard the last of that jar; my mistress was always throwing it in my face.

Some little time after this, one of the cows got loose from the stake, and eat one of the sweet-potatoe slips. I was milking when my master found it out. He came to me, and without any more ado, stooped down, and taking off his heavy boot, he struck me such a severe blow in the small of my back, that I shrieked with agony, and thought I was killed; and I feel a weakness in that part of this day. The cow was

frightened at his violence, and kicked down the pail and spilt the milk all about. My master knew that this accident was his own fault, but he was so enraged that he seemed glad of an excuse to go on with his ill usage. I cannot remember how many licks he gave me then, but he beat me till I was unable to stand, and till he himself was weary.

After this I ran away and went to my mother, who was living with Mr. Richard Darrel. My poor mother was both grieved and glad to see me; grieved because I had been so ill used, and glad because she had not seen me for a long, long while. She dared not receive me into the house, but she hid me up in a hole in the rocks near, and brought me food at night, after every body was asleep. My father, who lived at Crow-Lane, over the salt-water channel, at last heard of my being hid up in the cavern, and he came and took me back to my master. Oh I was loth, loth to go back; but as there was no remedy, I was obliged to submit.

When we got home, my poor father said to Capt. I--, "Sir, I am sorry that my child should be forced to run away from her owner; but the treatment she has received is enough to break her heart. The sight of her wounds has nearly broke mine.--I entreat you, for the love of God, to forgive her for running away, and that you will be a kind master to her in future." Capt. I--said I was used as well as I deserved, and that I ought to be punished for running away. I then took courage and said that I could stand the floggings no longer; that I was weary of my life, and therefore I had run away to my mother; but mothers could only weep and mourn over their children, they could not save them from cruel masters--from the whip, the rope, and the cowskin. He told me to hold my tongue and go about my work, or he would find a way to settle me. He did not, however, flog me that day.

For five years after this I remained in his house, and almost daily received the same harsh treatment. At length he put me on board a sloop, and to my great joy sent me away to Turk's Island. I was not permitted to see my mother or father, or poor sisters and brothers, to say good bye, though going away to a strange land, and might never see them again. Oh the Buckra people who keep slaves think that black people are like cattle, without natural affection. But my heart tells me it is far otherwise.

We were nearly four weeks on the voyage, which was unusually long. Sometimes we had a light breeze, sometimes a great calm, and the ship made no way; so that our provisions and water ran very low, and we were put upon short allowance. I should almost have been starved had it not been for the kindness of a black man called Anthony, and his wife, who had brought their own victuals, and shared them with me.

When we went ashore at the Grand Quay, the captain sent me to the house of my new master, Mr. D--, to whom Captain I--had sold me. Grand Quay is a small town upon a sandbank; the houses low and built of wood. Such was my new master's. The first person I saw, on my arrival, was Mr. D--, a stout sulky looking man, who carried me through the hall to show me to his wife and children. Next day I was put up by the vendue master to know how much I was worth, and I was valued at one hundred pounds currency.

My new master was one of the owners or holders of the salt ponds, and he received a certain sum for every slave that worked upon his premises, whether they were young or old. This sum was allowed him out of the profits arising from the salt works. I was immediately sent to work in the salt water with the rest of the slaves. This work was perfectly new to me. I was given a half barrel and a shovel, and had to stand up to my knees in the water, from four o'clock in the morning till nine, when we were given some Indian corn boiled in water, which we were obliged to swallow as fast as we could for fear the rain should come on and melt the salt. We were then called again to our tasks, and worked through the heat of the day; the sun flaming upon our heads like fire, and raising salt blisters in those parts which were not completely covered. Our feet and legs, from standing in the salt water for so many hours, soon became full of dreadful boils, which eat down in some cases to the very bone, afflicting the sufferers with great torment. We came home at twelve; ate our corn soup, called blawly , as fast as we could, and went back to our employment till dark at night. We then shovelled up the salt in large heaps, and went down to the sea, where we washed the pickle from our limbs, and cleaned the barrows and shovels from the salt. When we returned to the house, our master gave us each our allowance of raw Indian corn, which we pounded in a mortar and boiled in water for our suppers.

We slept in a long shed, divided into narrow slips, like the stalls used for cattle. Boards fixed upon stakes driven into the ground, without mat or covering, were our only beds. On Sundays, after we had washed the salt bags, and done other work required of us, we went into the bush and cut the long soft grass, of which we made trusses for our legs and feet to rest upon, for they were so full of the salt boils that we could get no rest lying upon the bare boards.

Though we worked from morning till night, there was no satisfying Mr. D--. I hoped, when I left Capt. I--, that I should have been better off, but I found it was but going from one butcher to another. There was this difference between them: my former master used to beat me while raging and foaming with passion; Mr. D--was usually quite calm. He would stand by and give orders for a slave to be cruelly whipped, and assist in the punishment, without moving a muscle of his face; walking about and taking snuff with the greatest composure. Nothing could touch his hard heart--neither sighs, nor tears, nor prayers, nor streaming blood; he was deaf to our cries, and careless of our sufferings.--Mr. D-- has often stripped me naked, hung me up by the wrists, and beat me with the cow-skin, with his own hand, till my body was raw with gashes. Yet there was nothing very remarkable in this; for it might serve as a sample of the common usage of the slaves on that horrible island.

Owing to the boils in my feet, I was unable to wheel the barrow fast through the sand, which got into the sores, and made me stumble at every step; and my master, having no pity for my sufferings from this cause, rendered them far more intolerable, by chastising me for not being able to move so fast as he wished me. Another of our employments was to row a little way off from the shore in a boat, and dive
for large stones to build a wall round our master's house. This was very hard work; and the great waves breaking over us continually, made us often so giddy that we lost our footing, and were in danger of being drowned.

Ah, poor me!--my tasks were never ended. Sick or well, it was work--work--work!--After the diving season was over, we were sent to the South Creek, with large bills, to cut up mangoes to burn lime with. Whilst one party of slaves were thus employed, another were sent to the other side of the island to break up coral out of the sea.

When we were ill, let our complaint be what it might, the only medicine given to us was a great bowl of hot salt water, with salt mixed with it, which made us very sick. If we could not keep up with the rest of the gang of slaves, we were put in the stocks, and severely flogged the next morning. Yet, not the less, our master expected, after we had thus been kept from our rest, and our limbs rendered stiff and sore with ill usage, that we should still go through the ordinary tasks of the day all the same.--Sometimes we had to work all night, measuring salt to load a vessel; or turning a machine to draw water out of the sea for the salt-making. Then we had no sleep--no rest--but were forced to work as fast as we could, and go on again all next day the same as usual. Work--work--work--Oh that Turk's Island was a horrible place! The people in England, I am sure, have never found out what is carried on there. Cruel, horrible place!

Mr. D-- had a slave called old Daniel, whom he used to treat in the most cruel manner. Poor Daniel was lame in the hip, and could not keep up with the rest of the slaves; and our master would order him to be stripped and laid down on the ground, and have him beaten with a rod of rough briar till his skin was quite red and raw. He would then call for a bucket of salt, and fling upon the raw flesh till the man writhed on the ground like a worm, and screamed aloud with agony. This poor man's wounds were never healed, and I have often seen them full of maggots, which increased his torments to an intolerable degree. He was an object of pity and terror to the whole gang of slaves, and in his wretched case we saw, each of us, our own lot, if we should live to be as old.

Oh the horrors of slavery!--How the thought of it pains my heart! But the truth ought to be told of it; and what my eyes have seen I think it is my duty to relate; for few people in England know what slavery is. I have been a slave--I have felt what a slave feels, and I know what a slave knows; and I would have all the good people in England to know it too, that they may break our chains, and set us free.

Mr. D-- had another slave called Ben. He being very hungry, stole a little rice one night after he came in from work, and cooked it for his supper. But his master soon discovered the theft; locked him up all night; and kept him without food till one o'clock the next day. He then hung Ben up by his hands, and beat him from time to time till the slaves came in at night. We found the poor creature hung up when we came home; with a pool of blood beneath him, and our master still licking him. But this was not the worst. My master's son was in the habit of stealing the rice and rum. Ben had seen him do this, and thought he might do the same, and when master found out that Ben had stolen the rice and swore to punish him, he tried to excuse himself by saying that Master Dickey did the same thing every night. The lad denied it to his father, and was so angry with Ben for inform- ing against him, that out of revenge he ran and got a bayonet, and whilst the poor wretch was suspended by his hands and writhing under his wounds, he run it quite through his foot. I was not by when he did it, but I saw the wound when I came home, and heard Ben tell the manner in which it was done.

I must say something more about this cruel son of a cruel fa- ther.--He had no heart--no fear of God; he had been brought up by a bad father in a bad path, and he delighted to follow in the same steps. There was a little old woman among the slaves called Sarah, who was nearly past work; and, Master Dickey being the overseer of the slaves just then, this poor creature, who was subject to several bodily infirmi- ties, and was not quite right in her head, did not wheel the barrow fast enough to please him. He threw her down on the ground, and after beating her severely, he took her up in his arms and flung her among the prickly-pear bushes, which are all covered over with sharp venomous prickles. By this her naked flesh was so grievously wounded, that her body swelled and festered all over, and she died a few days after. In telling my own sorrows, I cannot pass by those of my fellow-slaves--for when I think of my own griefs, I remember theirs.

I think it was about ten years I had worked in the salt ponds at Turk's Island, when my master left off business, and retired to a house he had in Bermuda, leaving his son to succeed him in the island. He took me with him to wait upon his daughters; and I was joyful, for I was sick, sick of Turk's Island, and my heart yearned to see my native place again, my mother, and my kindred.

I had seen my poor mother during the time I was a slave in Turk's Island. One Sunday morning I was on the beach with some of the slaves, and we saw a sloop come in loaded with slaves to work in the salt water. We got a boat and went aboard. When I came upon the deck I asked the black people, "Is there any one here for me?" "Yes," they said, "your mother." I thought they said this in jest--I could scarcely believe them for joy; but when I saw my poor mammy my joy was turned to sorrow, for she had gone from her senses. "Mammy," I said, "is this you?" She did not know me. "Mammy," I said, "what's the matter?" She began to talk foolishly, and said that she had been under the vessel's bottom. They had been overtaken by a violent storm at sea. My poor mother had never been on the sea before, and she was so ill, that she lost her senses, and it was long before she came quite to herself again. She had a sweet child with her--a little sister I had never seen, about four years of age, called Rebecca. I took her on shore with me, for I felt I should love her directly; and I kept her with me a week. Poor little thing! hers has been a sad life, and continues so to this day. My mother worked for some years on the island, but was taken back to Bermuda some time before my master carried me again thither.[‡‡]

[‡‡] Of the subsequent lot of her relatives she can tell but little. She says, her father died while she and her mother were at Turk's Island; and that he had been long dead and buried before any of his children in Bermuda knew of it, they being slaves on other estates. Her mother died after Mary went to Antigua. Of the fate of the rest of her kindred, seven brothers and three sisters, she

After I left Turk's Island, I was told by some negroes that came over from it, that the poor slaves had built up a place with boughs and leaves, where they might meet for prayers, but the white people pulled it down twice, and would not allow them even a shed for prayers. A flood came down soon after and washed away many houses, filled the place with sand, and overflowed the ponds: and I do think that this was for their wickedness; for the Buckra men[§§] I was several years the slave of Mr. D--after I returned to my native place. Here I worked in the grounds. My work was planting and hoeing sweet-potatoes, Indian corn, plantains, bananas, cabbages, pumpkins, onions, &c. I did all the household work, and attended upon a horse and cow besides,--going also upon all errands. I had to curry the horse--to clean and feed him-- and sometimes to ride him a little. I had more than enough to do--but still it was not so very bad as Turk's Island.

My old master often got drunk, and then he would get in a fury with his daughter, and beat her till she was not fit to be seen. I remember on one occasion, I had gone to fetch water, and when I was coming up the hill I heard a great screaming; I ran as fast as I could to the house, put down the water, and went into the chamber, where I found my master beating Miss D-- dreadfully. I strove with all my strength to get her away from him; for she was all black and blue with bruises. He had beat her with his fist, and almost killed her. The people gave me credit for getting her away. He turned round and began to lick me. Then I said, "Sir, this is not Turk's Island." I can't repeat his answer, the words were too wicked--too bad to say. He wanted to treat me the same in Bermuda as he had done in Turk's Island.

He had an ugly fashion of stripping himself quite naked, and ordering me then to wash him in a tub of water. This was worse to me than all the licks. Sometimes when he called me to wash him I would not come, my eyes were so full of shame. He would then come to beat me. One time I had plates and knives in my hand, and I dropped both plates and knives, and some of the plates were broken. He struck me

---

knows nothing further than this--that the eldest sister, who had several children to her master, was taken by him to Trinidad; and that the youngest, Rebecca, is still alive, and in slavery in Bermuda. Mary herself is now about forty-three years of age.-- Ed.

[§§] Negro term for white people. there were very wicked. I saw and heard much that was very very bad at that place.

so severely for this, that at last I defended myself, for I thought it was high time to do so. I then told him I would not live longer with him, for he was a very indecent man--very spiteful, and too indecent; with no shame for his servants, no shame for his own flesh. So I went away to a neighbouring house and sat down and cried till the next morning, when I went home again, not knowing what else to do.

After that I was hired to work at Cedar Hills, and every Saturday night I paid the money to my master. I had plenty of work to do there-- plenty of washing; but yet I made myself pretty comfortable. I earned two dollars and a quarter a week, which is twenty pence a day.

During the time I worked there, I heard that Mr. John Wood was going to Antigua. I felt a great wish to go there, and I went to Mr. D--, and asked him to let me go in Mr. Wood's service. Mr. Wood did not then want to purchase me; it was my own fault that I came under him, I was so anxious to go. It was ordained to be, I suppose; God led me there. The truth is, I did not wish to be any longer the slave of my in-decent master.

Mr. Wood took me with him to Antigua, to the town of St. John's, where he lived. This was about fifteen years ago. He did not then know whether I was to be sold; but Mrs. Wood found that I could work, and she wanted to buy me. Her husband then wrote to my mas-ter to inquire whether I was to be sold? Mr. D--wrote in reply, "that I should not be sold to any one that would treat me ill." It was strange he should say this, when he had treated me so ill himself. So I was pur-chased by Mr. Wood for 300 dollars, (or £100 Bermuda currency.)[***]

My work there was to attend the chambers and nurse the child, and to go down to the pond and wash clothes. But I soon fell ill of the rheumatism, and grew so very lame that I was forced to walk with a stick. I got the Saint Anthony's fire, also, in my left leg, and became quite a cripple. No one cared much to come near me, and I was ill a long long time; for several months I could not lift the limb. I had to lie in a little old out-house, that was swarming with bugs and other ver-min, which tormented me greatly; but I had no other place to lie in. I got the rheumatism by catching cold at the pond side, from washing in

---

[***]About £67. 10 s. sterling.

the fresh water; in the salt water I never got cold. The person who lived in next yard, (a Mrs. Greene,) could not bear to hear my cries and groans. She was kind, and used to send an old slave woman to help me, who sometimes brought me a little soup. When the doctor found I was so ill, he said I must be put into a bath of hot water. The old slave got the bark of some bush that was good for the pains, which she boiled in the hot water, and every night she came and put me into the bath, and did what she could for me: I don't know what I should have done, or what would have become of me, had it not been for her. --My mistress, it is true, did send me a little food; but no one from our family came near me but the cook, who used to shove my food in at the door, and say, "Molly, Molly, there's your dinner." My mistress did not care to take any trouble about me; and if the Lord had not put it into the hearts of the neighbours to be kind to me, I must, I really think, have lain and died.

It was a long time before I got well enough to work in the house. Mrs. Wood, in the meanwhile, hired a mulatto woman to nurse the child; but she was such a fine lady she wanted to be mistress over me. I thought it very hard for a coloured woman to have rule over me because I was a slave and she was free. Her name was Martha Wilcox; she was a saucy woman, very saucy; and she went and complained of me, without cause, to my mistress, and made her angry with me. Mrs. Wood told me that if I did not mind what I was about, she would get my master to strip me and give me fifty lashes: "You have been used to the whip," she said, "and you shall have it here." This was the first time she threatened to have me flogged; and she gave me the threatening so strong of what she would have done to me, that I thought I should have fallen down at her feet, I was so vexed and hurt by her words. The mulatto woman was rejoiced to have power to keep me down. She was constantly making mischief; there was no living for the slaves--no peace after she came.

I was also sent by Mrs. Wood to be put in the Cage one night, and was next morning flogged, by the magistrate's order, at her desire; and this all for a quarrel I had about a pig with another slave woman. I was flogged on my naked back on this occasion: although I was in no fault after all; for old Justice Dyett, when we came before him, said that I was in the right, and ordered the pig to be given to me. This was about two or three years after I came to Antigua.

40

When we moved from the middle of the town to the Point, I used to be in the house and do all the work and mind the children, though still very ill with the rheumatism. Every week I had to wash two large bundles of clothes, as much as a boy could help me to lift; but I could give no satisfaction. My mistress was always abusing and fretting after me. It is not possible to tell all her ill language.--One day she followed me foot after foot scolding and rating me. I bore in silence a great deal of ill words: at last my heart was quite full, and I told her that she ought not to use me so;--that when I was ill I might have lain and died for what she cared; and no one would then come near me to nurse me, because they were afraid of my mistress. This was a great affront. She called her husband and told him what I had said. He flew into a passion: but did not beat me then; he only abused and swore at me; and then gave me a note and bade me go and look for an owner. Not that he meant to sell me; but he did this to please his wife and to frighten me. I went to Adam White, a cooper, a free black, who had money, and asked him to buy me. He went directly to Mr. Wood, but was informed that I was not to be sold. The next day my master whipped me.

Another time (about five years ago) my mistress got vexed with me, because I fell sick and I could not keep on with my work. She complained to her husband, and he sent me off again to look for an owner. I went to a Mr. Burchell, showed him the note, and asked him to buy me for my own benefit; for I had saved about 100 dollars, and hoped, with a little help, to purchase my freedom. He accordingly went to my master:--"Mr. Wood," he said, "Molly has brought me a note that she wants an owner. If you intend to sell her, I may as well buy her as another." My master put him off and said that he did not mean to sell me. I was very sorry at this, for I had no comfort with Mrs. Wood, and I wished greatly to get my freedom.

The way in which I made my money was this.--When my master and mistress went from home, as they sometimes did, and left me to take care of the house and premises, I had a good deal of time to myself, and made the most of it. I took in washing, and sold coffee and yams
and other provisions to the captains of ships. I did not sit still idling during the absence of my owners; for I wanted, by all honest means, to earn money to buy my freedom. Sometimes I bought a hog cheap on board ship, and sold it for double the money on shore; and I

also earned a good deal by selling coffee. By this means I by degrees acquired a little cash. A gentleman also lent me some to help to buy my freedom--but when I could not get free he got it back again. His name was Captain Abbot.

My master and mistress went on one occasion into the country, to Date Hill, for change of air, and carried me with them to take charge of the children, and to do the work of the house. While I was in the country, I saw how the field negroes are worked in Antigua. They are worked very hard and fed but scantily. They are called out to work before daybreak, and come home after dark; and then each has to heave his bundle of grass for the cattle in the pen. Then, on Sunday morning, each slave has to go out and gather a large bundle of grass; and, when they bring it home, they have all to sit at the manager's door and wait till he come out: often have they to wait there till past eleven o'clock, without any breakfast. After that, those that have yams or potatoes, or fire-wood to sell, hasten to market to buy a dog's worth††† of salt fish, or pork, which is a great treat for them.

Some of them buy a little pickle out of the shad barrels, which they call sauce, to season their yams and Indian corn. It is very wrong, I know, to work on Sunday or go to market; but will not God call the Buckra men to answer for this on the great day of judgment--since they will give the slaves no other day?

While we were at Date Hill Christmas came; and the slave woman who had the care of the place (which then belonged to Mr. Roberts the marshal), asked me to go with her to her husband's house, to a Methodist meeting for prayer, at a plantation called Winthorps. I went; and they were the first prayers I ever understood. One woman prayed; and then they all sung a hymn; then there was another prayer and another hymn; and then they all spoke by turns of their own griefs as sinners. The husband of the woman I went with was a black driver. His name was Henry. He confessed that he had treated the slaves very cruelly; but said that he was compelled to obey the orders of his master. He prayed them all to forgive him, and he prayed that God would forgive him. He said it was a horrid thing for a ranger‡‡‡ to have some-

---

††† A dog is the 72nd part of a dollar.
‡‡‡ The head negro of an estate--a person who has the chief superintendence under the manager.

times to beat his own wife or sister; but he must do so if ordered by his master.

I felt sorry for my sins also. I cried the whole night, but I was too much ashamed to speak. I prayed God to forgive me. This meeting had a great impression on my mind, and led my spirit to the Moravian church; so that when I got back to town, I went and prayed to have my name put down in the Missionaries' book; and I followed the church earnestly every opportunity. I did not then tell my mistress about it; for I knew that she would not give me leave to go. But I felt I must go.

Whenever I carried the children their lunch at school, I ran round and went to hear the teachers.

The Moravian ladies (Mrs. Richter, Mrs. Olufsen, and Mrs. Sauter) taught me to read in the class; and I got on very fast. In this class there were all sorts of people, old and young, grey headed folks and children; but most of them were free people. After we had done spelling, we tried to read in the Bible. After the reading was over, the missionary gave out a hymn for us to sing. I dearly loved to go to the church, it was so solemn. I never knew rightly that I had much sin till I went there. When I found out that I was a great sinner, I was very sorely grieved, and very much frightened. I used to pray God to pardon my sins for Christ's sake, and forgive me for every thing I had done amiss; and when I went home to my work, I always thought about what I had heard from the missionaries, and wished to be good that I might go to heaven. After a while I was admitted a candidate for the holy Communion.--I had been baptized long before this, in August 1817, by the Rev. Mr. Curtin, of the English Church, after I had been taught to repeat the Creed and the Lord's Prayer. I wished at that time to attend a Sunday School taught by Mr. Curtin, but he would not receive me without a written note from my master, granting his permission. I did not ask my owner's permission, from the belief that it would be refused; so that I got no farther instruction at that time from the English Church.[§§§]

[§§§] She possesses a copy of Mrs. Trimmer's "Charity School Spelling Book," presented to her by the Rev. Mr. Curtin, and dated August 30, 1817. In this book her name is written "Mary, Princess of Wales"--an appellation which, she says, was given her by her owners. It is a common practice with the colonists to give ridiculous names of this description to their slaves; being, in fact,

Some time after I began to attend the Moravian Church, I met with Daniel James, afterwards my dear husband. He was a carpenter and cooper to his trade; an honest, hard-working, decent black man, and a widower. He had purchased his freedom of his mistress, old Mrs. Baker, with money he had earned whilst a slave. When he asked me to marry him, I took time to consider the matter over with myself, and would not say yes till he went to church with me and joined the Moravians. He was very industrious after he bought his freedom; and he had hired a comfortable house, and had convenient things about him. We were joined in marriage, about Christmas 1826, in the Moravian Chapel at Spring Gardens, by the Rev. Mr. Olufsen. We could not be married in the English Church. English marriage is not allowed to slaves; and no free man can marry a slave woman.

When Mr. Wood heard of my marriage, he flew into a great rage, and sent for Daniel, who was helping to build a house for his old mistress. Mr. Wood asked him who gave him a right to marry a slave of his? My husband said, "Sir, I am a free man, and thought I had a right to choose a wife; but if I had known Molly was not allowed to have a husband, I should not have asked her to marry me." Mrs. Wood was more vexed about my marriage than her husband. She could not forgive
me for getting married, but stirred up Mr. Wood to flog me dreadfully with the horsewhip. I thought it very hard to be whipped at my time of life for getting a husband--I told her so. She said that she would not have nigger men about the yards and premises, or allow a nigger man's clothes to be washed in the same tub where hers were washed. She was fearful, I think, that I should lose her time, in order to wash and do things for my husband: but I had then no time to wash for myself; I was obliged to put out my own clothes, though I was always at the wash-tub.

I had not much happiness in my marriage, owing to my being a slave. It made my husband sad to see me so ill-treated. Mrs. Wood was always abusing me about him. She did not lick me herself, but she got her husband to do it for her, whilst she fretted the flesh off my bones.

---

one of the numberless modes of expressing the habitual contempt with which they regard the negro race.--In printing this narrative we have retained Mary's paternal name of Prince.-- Ed.

Yet for all this she would not sell me. She sold five slaves whilst I was with her; but though she was always finding fault with me, she would not part with me. However, Mr. Wood afterwards allowed Daniel to have a place to live in our yard, which we were very thankful for.

After this, I fell ill again with the rheumatism, and was sick a long time; but whether sick or well, I had my work to do. About this time I asked my master and mistress to let me buy my own freedom. With the help of Mr. Burchell, I could have found the means to pay Mr. Wood; for it was agreed that I should afterwards serve Mr. Burchell a while, for the cash he was to advance for me. I was earnest in the request to my owners; but their hearts were hard--too hard to consent. Mrs. Wood was very angry--she grew quite outrageous--she called me a black devil, and asked me who had put freedom into my head. "To be free is very sweet," I said: but she took good care to keep me a slave. I saw her change colour, and I left the room.

About this time my master and mistress were going to England to put their son to school, and bring their daughters home; and they took me with them to take care of the child. I was willing to come to England: I thought that by going there I should probably get cured of my rheumatism, and should return with my master and mistress, quite well, to my husband. My husband was willing for me to come away, for he had heard that my master would free me,--and I also hoped this might prove true; but it was all a false report.

The steward of the ship was very kind to me. He and my husband were in the same class in the Moravian Church. I was thankful that he was so friendly, for my mistress was not kind to me on the passage; and she told me, when she was angry, that she did not intend to treat me any better in England than in the West Indies--that I need not expect it. And she was as good as her word.

When we drew near to England, the rheumatism seized all my limbs worse than ever, and my body was dreadfully swelled. When we landed at the Tower, I shewed my flesh to my mistress, but she took no great notice of it. We were obliged to stop at the tavern till my master got a house; and a day or two after, my mistress sent me down into the wash-house to learn to wash in the English way. In the West Indies we wash with cold water--in England with hot. I told my mistress I was afraid that putting my hands first into the hot water and then into

45

the cold, would increase the pain in my limbs. The doctor had told my mistress long before I came from the West Indies, that I was a sickly body and the washing did not agree with me. But Mrs. Wood would not release me from the tub, so I was forced to do as I could. I grew worse, and could not stand to wash. I was then forced to sit down with the tub before me, and often through pain and weakness was reduced to kneel or to sit down on the floor, to finish my task. When I complained to my mistress of this, she only got into a passion as usual, and said washing in hot water could not hurt any one;--that I was lazy and insolent, and wanted to be free of my work; but that she would make me do it. I thought her very hard on me, and my heart rose up within me. However I kept still at that time, and went down again to wash the child's things; but the English washerwomen who were at work there, when they saw that I was so ill, had pity upon me and washed them for me.

After that, when we came up to live in Leigh Street, Mrs. Wood sorted out five bags of clothes which we had used at sea, and also such as had been worn since we came on shore, for me and the cook to wash. Elizabeth the cook told her, that she did not think that I was able to stand to the tub, and that she had better hire a woman. I also said myself, that I had come over to nurse the child, and that I was sorry I had come from Antigua, since mistress would work me so hard, without compassion for my rheumatism. Mr. and Mrs. Wood, when they heard this, rose up in a passion against me. They opened the door and bade me get out. But I was a stranger, and did not know one door in the street from another, and was unwilling to go away. They made a dreadful uproar, and from that day they constantly kept cursing and abusing me. I was obliged to wash, though I was very ill. Mrs. Wood, indeed once hired a washerwoman, but she was not well treated, and would come no more.

My master quarrelled with me another time, about one of our great washings, his wife having stirred him up to do so. He said he would compel me to do the whole of the washing given out to me, or if I again refused, he would take a short course with me: he would either send me down to the brig in the river, to carry me back to Antigua, or he would turn me at once out of doors, and let me provide for myself. I said I would willingly go back, if he would let me purchase my own freedom. But this enraged him more than all the rest: he cursed and swore at me dreadfully, and said he would never sell my freedom--if I wished to be free, I was free in England, and I might go and try what freedom would do for me, and be d--d. My heart was very sore with this treatment, but I had to go on. I continued to do my work, and did all I could to give satisfaction, but all would not do.

Shortly after, the cook left them, and then matters went on ten times worse. I always washed the child's clothes without being commanded to do it, and any thing else that was wanted in the family; though still I was very sick--very sick indeed. When the great washing came round, which was every two months, my mistress got together again a great many heavy things, such as bed-ticks, bed-coverlets, &c. for me to wash. I told her I was too ill to wash such heavy things that day.

She said, she supposed I thought myself a free woman, but I was not; and if I did not do it directly I should be instantly turned out of doors. I stood a long time before I could answer, for I did not know well what to do. I knew that I was free in England, but I did not know where to go, or how to get my living; and therefore, I did not like to leave the house. But Mr. Wood said he would send for a constable to thrust me out; and at last I took courage and resolved that I would not be longer thus treated, but would go and trust to Providence. This was the fourth time they had threatened turn me out, and, go where I might, I was determined now to take them at their word; though I thought it very hard, after I had lived with them for thirteen years, and worked for them like a horse, to be driven out in this way, like a beggar. My only fault was being sick, and therefore unable to please my mistress, who thought she never could get work enough out of her slaves; and I told them so: but they only abused me and drove me out. This took place from two to three months, I think, after we came to England.

When I came away, I went to the man (one Mash) who used to black the shoes of the family, and asked his wife to get somebody to go with me to Hatton Garden to the Moravian Missionaries: these were the only persons I knew in England. The woman sent a young girl with me to the mission house, and I saw there a gentleman called Mr. Moore. I told him my whole story, and how my owners had treated me, and asked him to take in my trunk with what few clothes I had. The missionaries were very kind to me--they were sorry for my destitute situation, and gave me leave to bring my things to be placed under their care. They were very good people, and they told me to come to the church.

When I went back to Mr. Wood's to get my trunk, I saw a lady, Mrs. Pell, who was on a visit to my mistress. When Mr. and Mrs. Wood heard me come in, they set this lady to stop me, finding that they had gone too far with me. Mrs. Pell came out to me, and said, "Are you really going to leave, Molly? Don't leave, but come into the country with me." I believe she said this because she thought Mrs. Wood would easily get me back again. I replied to her, "Ma'am, this is the fourth time my master and mistress have driven me out, or threatened to drive me--and I will give them no more occasion to bid me go. I was not willing to leave them, for I am a stranger in this country, but now I must go--I can stay no longer to be so used." Mrs. Pell then went up stairs to my mistress, and told that I would go, and that she could not stop me. Mrs. Wood was very much hurt and frightened when she found I was determined to go out that day. She said, "If she goes the people will rob her, and then turn her adrift." She did not say this to me, but she spoke it loud enough for me to hear; that it might induce me not to go, I suppose. Mr. Wood also asked me where I was going to. I told him where I had been, and that I should never have gone away had I not been driven out by my owners. He had given me a written paper some time before, which said that I had come with them to England by my own desire; and that was true. It said also that I left them of my own free will, because I was a free woman in England; and that I was idle and would not do my work--which was not true. I gave this paper afterwards to a gentleman who inquired into my case. I went into the kitchen and got my clothes out. The nurse and the servant girl were there, and I said to the man who was going to take out my trunk, "Stop, before you take up this trunk, and hear what I have to say before these people. I am going out of this house, as I was ordered; but I have done no wrong at all to my owners, neither here nor in the West Indies. I always worked very hard to please them, both by night and day; but there was no giving satisfaction, for my mistress could never be satisfied with reasonable service. I told my mistress could never be satisfied with reasonable service. I told my mistress I was sick, and yet she has ordered me out of doors. This is the fourth time; and now I am going out."

And so I came out, and went and carried my trunk to the Moravians. I then returned back to Mash the shoe-black's house, and begged his wife to take me in. I had a little West Indian money in my trunk; and they got it changed for me. This helped to support me for a little while. The man's wife was very kind to me. I was very sick, and she boiled nourishing things up for me. She also sent for a doctor to see me, and he sent me medicine, which did me good, though I was ill for a long time with the rheumatic pains. I lived a good many months with these poor people, and they nursed me, and did all that lay in their power to serve me. The man was well acquainted with my situation, as he used to go to and fro to Mr. Wood's house to clean shoes and knives; and he and his wife were sorry for me.

About this time, a woman of the name of Hill told me of the Anti-Slavery Society, and went with me to their office, to inquire if they could do anything to get me my freedom, and send me back to the West Indies. The gentlemen of the Society took me to a lawyer, who examined very strictly into my case; but told me that the laws of England could do nothing to make me free in Antigua. [****]

However they did all they could for me: they gave me a little money from time to time to keep me from want; and some of them went to Mr. Wood to try to persuade him to let me return a free woman to my husband; but though they offered him, as I have heard, a large sum for my freedom, he was sulky and obstinate, and would not consent to let me go free.

This was the first winter I spent in England, and I suffered much from the severe cold, and from the rheumatic pains, which still at times torment me. However, Providence was very good to me, and I got many friends--especially some Quaker ladies, who hearing of my case, came and sought me out, and gave me good warm clothing and money. Thus I had great cause to bless God in my affliction.

When I got better I was anxious to get some work to do, as I was unwilling to eat the bread of idleness. Mrs. Mash, who was a laundress, recommended me to a lady for a charwoman. She paid me very handsomely for what work I did, and I divided the money with Mrs. Mash;

for though very poor, they gave me food when my own money was done, and never suffered me to want.

[****] She came first to the Anti-Slavery Office in Aldermanbury, about the latter end of November 1828; and her case was referred to Mr. George Stephen to be investigated. More of this hereafter.-- Ed .

In the spring, I got into service with a lady, who saw me at the house where I sometimes worked as a charwoman. This lady's name was Mrs. Forsyth. She had been in the West Indies, and was accustomed to Blacks, and liked them. I was with her six months, and went with her to Margate. She treated me well, and gave me a good character when she left London.

After Mrs. Forsyth went away, I was again out of place, and went to lodgings, for which I paid two shillings a week, and found coals and candle. After eleven weeks, the money I had saved in service was all gone, and I was forced to go back to the Anti-Slavery office to ask a supply, till I could get another situation. I did not like to go back--I did not like to be idle. I would rather work for my living than get it for nothing. They were very good to give me a supply, but I felt shame at being obliged to apply for relief whilst I had strength to work.

At last I went into the service of Mr. and Mrs. Pringle, where I have been ever since, and am as comfortable as I can be while separated from my dear husband, and away from my own country and all old friends and connections. My dear mistress teaches me daily to read the word of God, and takes great pains to make me understand it. I enjoy the great privilege of being enabled to attend church three times on the Sunday: and I have met with many kind friends since I have been here, both clergymen and others. The Rev. Mr. Young, who lives in the next house, has shown me much kindness, and taken much pains to instruct me, particularly while my master and mistress were absent in Scotland. Nor must I forget, among my friends, the Rev. Mr. Mortimer, the good clergyman of the parish, under whose ministry I have now sat for upwards of twelve months. I trust in God I have profited by what I have heard from him. He never keeps back the truth, and I think he has been the means of opening my eyes and ears much better to understand the word of God. Mr. Mortimer tells me that he cannot open the eyes of my heart, but that I must pray to God to change my heart, and make me to know the truth, and the truth will make me free.

I still live in the hope that God will find a way to give me my liberty, and give me back to my husband. I endeavour to keep down my fretting, and to leave all to Him, for he knows what is good for me better than I know myself. Yet, I must confess, I find it a hard and heavy task to do so.

I am often much vexed, and I feel great sorrow when I hear some people in this country say, that the slaves do not need better usage, and do not want to be free.^{††††} They believe the foreign people,^{‡‡‡‡} who deceive them, and say slaves are happy. I say, Not so. How can slaves be happy when they have the halter round their neck and the whip upon their back? and are disgraced and thought no more of than beasts?--and are separated from their mothers, and husbands, and children, and sisters, just as cattle are sold and separated? Is it happiness for a driver in the field to take down his wife or sister or child, and strip them, and whip them in such a disgraceful manner?--women that have had children exposed in the open field to shame! There is no modesty or decency shown by the owner to his slaves; men, women, and children are exposed alike. Since I have been here I have often wondered how English people can go out into the West Indies and act in such a beastly manner. But when they go to the West Indies, they forget God and all feeling of shame, I think, since they can see and do such things. They tie up slaves like hogs--moor^{§§§§} them up like cattle, and they lick them, so as hogs, or cattle, or horses never were flogged;--and yet they come home and say, and make some good people believe, that slaves don't want to get out of slavery. But they put a cloak about the truth. It is not so. All slaves want to be free--to be free is very sweet. I will say the truth to English people who may read this history that my good friend, Miss S--, is now writing down for me. I have been a slave myself--I know what slaves feel--I can tell by myself what other slaves feel, and by what they have told me. The man that says slaves be quite happy in slavery--that they don't want to be free--that man is either ignorant or a lying person. I never heard a slave say so. I never heard a Buckra man say so, till I heard tell of it in England. Such people ought to be ashamed of themselves. They can't do without slaves, they say. What's the reason they can't do without slaves as well as in England? No slaves here--no whips--no stocks--no punishment, except for wicked people. They hire servants in England; and if they don't like them, they send them away: they can't lick them. Let them work ever so hard in England, they are far better off than slaves. If they get a bad master, they give warning and go hire to another. They have their liberty. That's just what we want. We don't

---

^{††††} The whole of this paragraph especially, is given as nearly as was possible in Mary's precise words.
^{‡‡‡‡} She means West Indians.
^{§§§§} A West Indian phrase: to fasten or tie up.

mind hard work, if we had proper treatment, and proper wages like English servants, and proper time given in the week to keep us from breaking the Sabbath. But they won't give it: they will have work--work--work, night and day, sick or well, till we are quite done up; and we must not speak up nor look amiss, however much we be abused. And then when we are quite done up, who cares for us, more than for a lame horse? This is slavery. I tell it, to let English people know the truth; and I hope they will never leave off to pray God, and call loud to the great King of England, till all the poor blacks be given free, and slavery done up for evermore.

The narrative of Sojourner Truth

HER BIRTH AND PARENTAGE

The subject of this biography, SOJOURNER TRUTH, as she now calls herself–but whose name, originally, was Isabella–was born, as near as she can now calculate, between the years 1797 and 1800. She was the daughter of James and Betsey, slaves of one Colonel Ardinburgh, Hurley, Ulster County, New York.

Colonel Ardinburgh belonged to that class of people called Low Dutch.

Of her first master, she can give no account, as she must have been a mere infant when he died; and she, with her parents and some ten or twelve other fellow human chattels, became the legal property of his son, Charles Ardinburgh. She distinctly remembers hearing her father and mother say, that their lot was a fortunate one, as Master Charles was the best of the family,–being, comparatively speaking, a kind master to his slaves.

James and Betsey having, by their faithfulness, docility, and respectful behavior, won his particular regard, received from him particular favors–among which was a lot of land, lying back on the slope of a mountain, where, by improving the pleasant evenings and Sundays, they managed to raise a little tobacco, corn, or flax; which they exchanged for extras, in the articles of food or clothing for themselves and children. She has no remembrance that Saturday afternoon was ever added to their own time, as it is by some masters in the Southern States.

ACCOMMODATIONS

Among Isabella's earliest recollections was the removal of her master, Charles Ardinburgh, into his new house, which he had built for a hotel, soon after the decease of his father. A cellar, under this hotel, was assigned to his slaves, as their sleeping apartment,–all the slaves he possessed, of both sexes, sleeping (as is quite common in a state of slavery) in the same room. She carries in her mind, to this day, a vivid picture of this dismal chamber; its only lights consisting of a few panes of glass, through which she thinks the sun never shone, but with thrice reflected rays; and the space between the loose boards of the floor, and the uneven earth below, was often filled with mud and water, the uncomfortable splashings of which were as annoying as its noxious vapors must have been chilling and fatal to health. She shudders, even now, as she goes back in memory, and revisits this cellar, and sees its inmates, of both sexes and all ages, sleeping on those damp boards, like the horse, with a little straw and a blanket; and she wonders not at the rheumatisms, and fever-sores, and palsies, that distorted the limbs and racked the bodies of those fellow-slaves in after-life. Still, she does not attribute this cruelty–for cruelty it certainly is, to be so unmindful of the health and comfort of any being, leaving entirely out of sight his more important part, his everlasting interests,–so much to any innate or constitutional cruelty of the master, as to that gigantic inconsistency, that inherited habit among slaveholders, of expecting a willing and intelligent obedience from the slave, because he is a MAN–at the same time every thing belonging to the soul-harrowing system does its best to crush the last vestige of a man within him; and when it is crushed, and often before, he is denied the comforts of life, on the plea that he knows neither the want nor the use of them, and because he is considered to be little more or little less than a beast.

HER BROTHERS AND SISTERS

Isabella's father was very tall and straight, when young, which gave him the name of 'Bomefree'–low Dutch for tree–at least, this is SOJOURNER's pronunciation of it–and by this name he usually went. The most familiar appellation of her mother was 'Mau-mau Bett.' She was the mother of some ten or twelve children; though Sojourner is far from knowing the exact number of her brothers and sisters; she being the youngest, save one, and all older than herself having been sold before her remembrance. She was privileged to behold six of them while she remained a slave.

Of the two that immediately preceded her in age, a boy of five years, and a girl of three, who were sold when she was an infant, she heard much; and she wishes that all who would fain believe that slave parents have not natural affection for their offspring could have listened as she did, while Bomefree and Mau-mau Bett,–their dark cellar lighted by a blazing pine-knot,–would sit for hours, recalling and recounting every endearing, as well as harrowing circumstance that taxed memory could supply, from the histories of those dear departed ones, of whom they had been robbed, and for whom their hearts still bled. Among the rest, they would relate how the little boy, on the last morning he was with them, arose with the birds, kindled a fire, calling for his Mau-mau to 'come, for all was now ready for her'–little dreaming of the dreadful separation which was so near at hand, but of which his parents had an uncertain, but all the more cruel foreboding. There was snow on the ground, at the time of which we are speaking; and a large old-fashioned sleigh was seen to drive up to the door of the late Col. Ardinburgh. This event was noticed with childish pleasure by the unsuspicious boy; but when he was taken and put into the sleigh, and saw his little sister actually shut and locked into the sleigh box, his eyes were at once opened to their intentions; and, like a frightened deer he sprang from the sleigh, and running into the house, concealed himself under a bed. But this availed him little. He was re-conveyed to the sleigh, and separated for ever from those whom God had constituted his natural guardians and protectors, and who should have found him, in return, a stay and a staff to them in their declining years. But I make no comments on facts like these, knowing that the heart of every slave parent will make its own comments, involuntarily and correctly, as soon as each heart shall make the case its own. Those who are not parents will draw their conclusions from the promptings of humanity and philanthropy:–these, enlightened by reason and revelation, are also unerring.

HER RELIGIOUS INSTRUCTION

Isabella and Peter, her youngest brother, remained, with their parents, the legal property of Charles Ardinburgh till his decease, which took place when Isabella was near nine years old.

After this event, she was often surprised to find her mother in tears; and when, in her simplicity, she inquired, 'Mau-mau, what makes you cry?' she would answer, 'Oh, my child, I am thinking of your brothers and sisters that have been sold away from me.' And she would proceed to detail many circumstances respecting them. But Isabella long since concluded that it was the impending fate of her only remaining children, which her mother but too well understood, even then, that called up those memories from the past, and made them crucify her heart afresh.

In the evening, when her mother's work was done, she would sit down under the sparkling vault of heaven, and calling her children to her, would talk to them of the only Being that could effectually aid or protect them. Her teachings were delivered in Low Dutch, her only language, and, translated into English, ran nearly as follows:-

'My children, there is a God, who hears and sees you.' 'A God, mau-mau! Where does he live?' asked the children. 'He lives in the sky,' she replied; 'and when you are beaten, or cruelly treated, or fall into any trouble, you must ask help of him, and he will always hear and help you.' She taught them to kneel and say the Lord's Prayer. She entreated them to refrain from lying and stealing, and to strive to obey their masters.

At times, a groan would escape her, and she would break out in the language of the Psalmist–'Oh Lord, how long?' 'Oh Lord, how long?' And in reply to Isabella's question–'What ails you, mau-mau?' her only answer was, 'Oh, a good deal ails me'–'Enough ails me.' Then again, she would point them to the stars, and say, in her peculiar language, 'Those are the same stars, and that is the same moon, that look down upon your brothers and sisters, and which they see as they look up to them, though they are ever so far away from us, and each other.'

Thus, in her humble way, did she endeavor to show them their Heavenly Father, as the only being who could protect them in their perilous condition; at the same time, she would strengthen and brighten the chain of family affection, which she trusted extended itself sufficiently to connect the widely scattered members of her precious flock. These instructions of the mother were treasured up and held sacred by Isabella, as our future narrative will show.

THE AUCTION

At length, the never-to-be-forgotten day of the terrible auction arrived, when the 'slaves, horses, and other cattle' of Charles Ardinburgh, deceased, were to be put under the hammer, and again change masters. Not only Isabella and Peter, but their mother, were now destined to the auction block, and would have been struck off with the rest to the highest bidder, but for the following circumstance: A question arose among the heirs, 'Who shall be burdened with Bomefree, when we have sent away his faithful Mau-mau Bett?' He was becoming weak and infirm; his limbs were painfully rheumatic and distorted– more from exposure and hardship than from old age, though he was several years older than Mau-mau Bett: he was no longer considered of value, but must soon be a burden and care to some one. After some contention on the point at issue, none being willing to be burdened with him, it was finally agreed, as most expedient for the heirs, that the price of Mau-mau Bett should be sacrificed, and she receive her freedom, on condition that she take care of and support her faithful James,– faithful, not only to her as a husband, but proverbially faithful as a slave to those who would not willingly sacrifice a dollar for his comfort, now that he had commenced his descent into the dark vale of decrepitude and suffering. This important decision was received as joyful news indeed to our ancient couple, who were the objects of it, and who were trying to prepare their hearts for a severe struggle, and one altogether new to them, as they had never before been separated; for, though ignorant, helpless, crushed in spirit, and weighed down with hardship and cruel bereavement, they were still human, and their human hearts beat within them with as true an affection as ever caused a human heart to beat. And their anticipated separation now, in the decline of life, after the last child had been torn from them, must have been truly appalling. Another privilege was granted them–that of remaining occupants of the same dark, humid cellar I have before described: otherwise, they were to support themselves as they best could. And as her mother was still able to do considerable work, and her father a little, they got on for some time very comfortably. The strangers who rented the house were humane people, and very kind to them; they were not rich, and owned no slaves. How long this state of things continued, we are unable to say, as Isabella had not then sufficiently cultivated her organ of time to calculate years, or even weeks or hours. But she thinks her mother must have lived several years after the death of Master Charles. She remembers going to visit her parents some three or four times before the death of her mother, and a good deal of time seemed to her to intervene between each visit.

At length her mother's health began to decline–a fever-sore made its ravages on one of her limbs, and the palsy began to shake her frame; still, she and James tottered about, picking up a little here and there, which, added to the mites contributed by their kind neighbors, sufficed to sustain life, and drive famine from the door.

DEATH OF MAU-MAU BETT

One morning, in early autumn, (from the reason above mentioned, we cannot tell what year,) Mau-mau Bett told James she would make him a loaf of rye-bread, and get Mrs. Simmons, their kind neighbor, to bake it for them, as she would bake that forenoon. James told her he had engaged to rake after the cart for his neighbors that morning; but before he commenced, he would pole off some apples from a tree near, which they were allowed to gather; and if she could get some of them baked with the bread, it would give a nice relish for their dinner. He beat off the apples, and soon after, saw Mau-mau Bett come out and gather them up.

At the blowing of the horn for dinner, he groped his way into his cellar, anticipating his humble, but warm and nourishing meal; when, lo! instead of being cheered by the sight and odor of fresh-baked bread and the savory apples, his cellar seemed more cheerless than usual, and at first neither sight nor sound met eye or ear. But, on groping his way through the room, his staff, which he used as a pioneer to go before, and warn him of danger, seemed to be impeded in its progress, and a low, gurgling, choking sound proceeded from the object before him, giving him the first intimation of the truth as it was, that Mau-mau Bett, his bosom companion, the only remaining member of his large family, had fallen in a fit of the palsy, and lay helpless and senseless on the earth! Who among us, located in pleasant homes, surrounded with every comfort, and so many kind and sympathizing friends, can picture to ourselves the dark and desolate state of poor old James–penniless, weak, lame, and nearly blind, as he was at the moment he found his companion was removed from him, and he was left alone in the world, with no one to aid, comfort, or console him? for she never revived again, and lived only a few hours after being discovered senseless by her poor bereaved James.

LAST DAYS OF BOMEFREE

Isabella and Peter were permitted to see the remains of their mother laid in their last narrow dwelling, and to make their bereaved father a little visit, ere they returned to their servitude. And most piteous were the lamentations of the poor old man, when, at last, they also were obliged to bid him "Farewell!" Juan Fernandes, on his desolate island, was not so pitiable an object as this poor lame man. Blind and crippled, he was too superannuated to think for a moment of taking care of himself, and he greatly feared no persons would interest themselves in his behalf. 'Oh,' he would exclaim, 'I had thought God would take me first,–Mau-mau was so much smarter than I, and could get about and take care of herself;–and I am so old, and so helpless. What is to become of me? I can't do anything any more–my children are all gone, and here I am left helpless and alone.' 'And then, as I was taking leave of him,' said his daughter, in relating it, 'he raised his voice, and cried aloud like a child–Oh, how he DID cry! I HEAR it now –and remember it as well as if it were but yesterday–poor old man!!! He thought God had done it all–and my heart bled within me at the sight of his misery. He begged me to get permission to come and see him sometimes, which I readily and heartily promised him.' But when all had left him, the Ardinburghs, having some feeling left for their faithful and favorite slave, 'took turns about' in keeping him– permitting him to stay a few weeks at one house, and then a while at another, and so around. If, when he made a removal, the place where he was going was not too far off, he took up his line of march, staff in hand, and asked for no assistance. If it was twelve or twenty miles, they gave him a ride. While he was living in this way, Isabella was twice permitted to visit him. Another time she walked twelve miles, and carried her infant in her arms to see him, but when she reached the place where she hoped to find him, he had just left for a place some twenty miles distant, and she never saw him more. The last time she did see him, she found him seated on a rock, by the road side, alone, and far from any house. He was then migrating from the house of one Ardinburgh to that of another, several miles distant. His hair was white like wool– he was almost blind–and his gait was more a creep than a walk–but the weather was warm and pleasant, and he did not dislike the journey. When Isabella addressed him, he recognized her voice, and was exceeding glad to see her. He was assisted to mount the wagon, was carried back to the famous cellar of which we have spoken, and there they held their last earthly conversation. He again, as usual, bewailed his loneliness,–spoke in tones of anguish of his many children, saying, "They are all taken away from me! I have now not one to give me a cup of cold water–why should I live and not die?" Isabella, whose heart yearned over her father, and who would have made any sacrifice to have been able to be with, and take care of him, tried to comfort, by telling him that 'she had heard the white folks say, that all the slaves in the State would be freed in ten years, and that then she would come and take care of him.' 'I would take just as good care of you as Maumau would, if she was here'–continued Isabel. 'Oh, my child,' replied he, 'I cannot live that long.' 'Oh, do, daddy, do live, and I will take such good care of you,' was her rejoinder. She now says, 'Why, I thought then, in my ignorance, that he could live, if he would. I just as much thought so, as I ever thought any thing in my life–and I insisted on his living: but he shook his head, and insisted he could not.'

But before Bomefree's good constitution would yield either to age, exposure, or a strong desire to die, the Ardinburghs again tired of him, and offered freedom to two old slaves–Caesar, brother of Mau-mau Bett, and his wife Betsy–on condition that they should take care of James. (I was about to say, 'their brother-in-law'–but as slaves are neither husbands nor wives in law, the idea of their being brothers-in-law is truly ludicrous.) And although they were too old and infirm to take care of themselves, (Caesar having been afflicted for a long time with fever-sores, and his wife with the jaundice), they eagerly accepted the boon of freedom, which had been the life-long desire of their souls–though at a time when emancipation was to them little more than destitution, and was a freedom more to be desired by the master than the slave. Sojourner declares of the slaves in their ignorance, that 'their thoughts are no longer than her finger.'

DEATH OF BOMEFREE

A rude cabin, in a lone wood, far from any neighbors, was granted to our freed friends, as the only assistance they were now to expect. Bomefree, from this time, found his poor needs hardly supplied, as his new providers were scarce able to administer to their own wants. However, the time drew near when things were to be decidedly worse rather than better; for they had not been together long, before Betty died, and shortly after, Caesar followed her to 'that bourne from whence no traveler returns'–leaving poor James again desolate, and more helpless than ever before; as, this time, there was no kind family in the house, and the Ardinburghs no longer invited him to their homes. Yet, lone, blind and helpless as he was, James for a time lived on. One day, an aged colored woman, named Soan, called at his shanty, and James besought her, in the most moving manner, even with tears, to tarry awhile and wash and mend him up, so that he might once more be decent and comfortable; for he was suffering dreadfully with the filth and vermin that had collected upon him.

Soan was herself an emancipated slave, old and weak, with no one to care for her; and she lacked the courage to undertake a job of such seeming magnitude, fearing she might herself get sick, and perish there without assistance; and with great reluctance, and a heart swelling with pity, as she afterwards declared, she felt obliged to leave him in his wretchedness and filth. And shortly after her visit, this faithful slave, this deserted wreck of humanity, was found on his miserable pallet, frozen and stiff in death. The kind angel had come at last, and relieved him of the many miseries that his fellow-man had heaped

60

upon him. Yes, he had died, chilled and starved, with none to speak a kindly word, or do a kindly deed for him, in that last dread of hour of need!

The news of his death reached the ears of John Ardinburgh, a grandson of the old Colonel; and he declared that 'Bomefree, who had ever been a kind and faithful slave, should now have a good funeral.' And now, gentle reader, what think you constituted a good funeral? Answer–some black paint for the coffin, and–a jug of ardent spirits! What a compensation for a life of toil, of patient submission to repeated robberies of the most aggravated kind, and, also, far more than murderous neglect!! Mankind often vainly attempts to atone for unkindness or cruelty to the living, by honoring the same after death; but John Ardinburgh undoubtably meant his pot of paint and jug of whisky should act as an opiate on his slaves, rather than on his own seared conscience.

COMMENCEMENT OF ISABELLA'S TRIALS IN LIFE

Having seen the sad end of her parents, so far as it relates to this earthly life, we will return with Isabella to that memorable auction which threatened to separate her father and mother. A slave auction is a terrible affair to its victims, and its incidents and consequences are graven on their hearts as with a pen of burning steel.

At this memorable time, Isabella was struck off, for the sum of one hundred dollars, to one John Nealy, of Ulster County, New York; and she has an impression that in this sale she was connected with a lot of sheep. She was now nine years of age, and her trials in life may be dated from this period. She says, with emphasis, 'Now the war begun. ' She could only talk Dutch–and the Nealys could only talk English. Mr. Nealy could understand Dutch, but Isabel and her mistress could neither of them understand the language of the other–and this, of itself, was a formidable obstacle in the way of a good understanding between them, and for some time was a fruitful source of dissatisfaction to the mistress, and of punishment and suffering to Isabella. She says, 'If they sent me for a frying-pan, not knowing what they meant, perhaps I carried them pot-hooks and trammels. Then, oh! how angry mistress would be with me!' Then she suffered 'terribly–terribly ', with the cold. During the winter her feet were badly frozen, for want of proper covering. They gave her a plenty to eat, and also a plenty of whippings. One Sunday morning, in particular, she was told to go to the barn; on going there, she found her master with a bundle of rods, prepared in the embers, and bound together with cords. When he had tied her hands together before her, he gave her the most cruel whipping she was ever tortured with. He whipped her till the flesh was deeply lacerated, and the blood streamed from her wounds–and the scars remain to the present day, to testify to the fact. 'And now,' she says, 'when I hear 'em tell of whipping women on the bare flesh, it makes my flesh crawl, and my very hair rise on my head! Oh! my God!' she continues, 'what a way is this of treating human beings?' In those hours of her extremity, she did not forget the instructions of her mother, to go to God in all her trials, and every affliction; and she not only remembered, but obeyed: going to him, 'and telling him all–and asking Him if He thought it was right,' and begging him to protect and shield her from her persecutors.

She always asked with an unwavering faith that she should receive just what she pleaded for,–'And now,' she says, 'though it seems curious, I do not remember ever asking for any thing but what I got it. And I always received it as an answer to my prayers. When I got beaten, I never knew it long enough to go beforehand to pray; and I always thought that if I only had had time to pray to God for help, I should have escaped the beating.' She had no idea God had any knowledge of her thoughts, save what she told him; or heard her prayers, unless they were spoken audibly. And consequently, she could not pray unless she had time and opportunity to go by herself, where she could talk to God without being overheard.

TRIALS CONTINUED

When she had been at Mr. Nealy's several months, she began to beg God most earnestly to send her father to her, and as soon as she commenced to pray, she began as confidently to look for his coming, and, ere it was long, to her great joy, he came. She had no opportunity to speak to him of the troubles that weighed so heavily on her spirit, while he remained; but when he left, she followed him to the gate, and unburdened her heart to him, inquiring if he could not do something to get her a new and better place. In this way the slaves often assist each other, by ascertaining who are kind to their slaves, comparatively; and then using their influence to get such an one to hire or buy their friends; and masters, often from policy, as well as from latent humanity, allow those they are about to sell or let, to choose their own places, if the persons they happen to select for masters are considered safe pay. He promised to do all he could, and they parted. But, every day, as long as the snow lasted, (for there was snow on the ground at the time,) she returned to the spot where they separated, and walking in the tracks her father had made in the snow, repeated her prayer that 'God would help her father get her a new and better place.'

A long time had not elapsed, when a fisherman by the name of Scriver appeared at Mr. Nealy's, and inquired of Isabel 'if she would like to go and live with him.' She eagerly answered 'Yes,' and nothing doubting but he was sent in answer to her prayer; and she soon started off with him, walking while he rode; for he had bought her at the suggestion of her father, paying one hundred and five dollars for her. He also lived in Ulster County, but some five or six miles from Mr. Nealy's.

Scriver, besides being a fisherman, kept a tavern for the accommodation of people of his own class—for his was a rude, uneducated family, exceedingly profane in their language, but, on the whole, an honest, kind and well-disposed people.

They owned a large farm, but left it wholly unimproved; attending mainly to their vocations of fishing and inn-keeping. Isabella declares she can ill describe the kind of life she led with them. It was a wild, out-of-door kind of life. She was expected to carry fish, to hoe corn, to bring roots and herbs from the woods for beers, go to the Strand for a gallon of molasses or liquor as the case might require, and 'browse around,' as she expresses it. It was a life that suited her well for the time-being as devoid of hardship or terror as it was of improvement; a need which had not yet become a want. Instead of improving at this place, morally, she retrograded, as their example taught her to curse; and it was here that she took her first oath. After living with them for about a year and a half, she was sold to one John J. Dumont, for the sum of seventy pounds. This was in 1810. Mr. Dumont lived in the same county as her former masters, in the town of New Paltz, and she remained with him till a short time previous to her emancipation by the State, in 1828.

HER STANDING WITH HER NEW MASTER AND MISTRESS

Had Mrs. Dumont possessed that vein of kindness and consideration for the slaves, so perceptible in her husband's character, Isabella would have been as comfortable here, as one had best be, if one must be a slave. Mr. Dumont had been nursed in the very lap of slavery, and being naturally a man of kind feelings, treated his slaves with all the consideration he did his other animals, and more, perhaps.

But Mrs. Dumont, who had been born and educated in a non-slaveholding family, and, like many others, used only to work-people, who, under the most stimulating of human motives, were willing to put forth their every energy, could not have patience with the creeping gait, the dull understanding, or see any cause for the listless manners and careless, slovenly habits of the poor down-trodden outcast– entirely forgetting that every high and efficient motive had been re-moved far from him; and that, had not his very intellect been crushed out of him, the slave would find little ground for aught but hopeless despondency. From this source arose a long series of trials in the life of our heroine, which we must pass over in silence; some from motives of delicacy, and others, because the relation of them might inflict undeserved pain on some now living, whom Isabel remembers only with esteem and love; therefore, the reader will not be surprised if our narrative appears somewhat tame at this point, and may rest assured that it is not for want of facts, as the most thrilling incidents of this portion of her life are from various motives suppressed.

One comparatively trifling incident she wishes related, as it made a deep impression on her mind at the time-showing, as she thinks, how God shields the innocent, and causes them to triumph over their enemies, and also how she stood between master and mistress. In her family, Mrs. Dumont employed two white girls, one of whom, named Kate, evinced a disposition to 'lord it over' Isabel, and, in her emphatic language, 'to grind her down '. Her master often shielded her from the attacks and accusations of others, praising her for her readiness and ability to work, and these praises seemed to foster a spirit of hostility to her, in the minds of Mrs. Dumont and her white servant, the latter of whom took every opportunity to cry up her faults, lessen her in the esteem of her master and increase against her the displeasure of her mistress, which was already more than sufficient for Isabel's comfort. Her master insisted that she could do as much work as half a dozen common people, and do it well, too; whilst her mistress insisted that the first was true, only because it ever came from her hand but half performed. A good deal of feeling arose from this difference of opinion, which was getting to rather an uncomfortable height, when, all at once, the potatoes that Isabel cooked for breakfast assumed a dingy, dirty look. Her mistress blamed her severely, asking her master to observe 'a fine specimen of Bell's work!'–adding, 'it is the way all her work is done.' Her master scolded also this time, and commanded her to be more careful in future. Kate joined with zest in the censures, and was very hard upon her. Isabella thought that she had done all she well could to have them nice; and became quite distressed at their appearances, and wondered what she should do to avoid them. In this dilemma, Gertrude Dumont (Mr. D.'s eldest child, a good, kind-hearted girl of ten years, who pitied Isabel sincerely), when she heard them all blame her so unsparingly, came forward, offering her sympathy and assistance; and when about to retire to bed, on the night of Isabella's humiliation, she advanced to Isabel, and told her, if she would wake her early next morning, she would get up and attend to her potatoes for her, while she (Isabella) went to milking, and they would see if they could not have them nice, and not have 'Poppee,' her word for father, and 'Matty,' her word for mother, and all of 'em, scolding so terribly.

Isabella gladly availed herself of this kindness, which touched her to the heart, amid so much of an opposite spirit. When Isabella had put the potatoes over to boil, Getty told her she would herself tend the fire, while Isabel milked. She had not long been seated by the fire, in performance of her promise, when Kate entered, and requested Gertrude to go out of the room and do something for her, which she refused, still keeping her place in the corner. While there, Kate came sweeping about the fire, caught up a chip, lifted some ashes with it, and dashed them into the kettle. Now the mystery was solved, the plot discovered! Kate was working a little too fast at making her mistress's words good, at showing that Mrs. Dumont and herself were on the right side of the dispute, and consequently at gaining power over Isabella. Yes, she was quite too fast, inasmuch as she had overlooked the little figure of justice, which sat in the comer, with scales nicely balanced, waiting to give all their dues.

But the time had come when she was to be overlooked no longer. It was Getty's turn to speak now. 'Oh Poppee! oh Poppee!' said she, 'Kate has been putting ashes in among the potatoes! I saw her do it! Look at those that fell on the outside of the kettle! You can now see what made the potatoes so dingy every morning, though Bell washed them clean!' And she repeated her story to every new comer, till the fraud was made as public as the censure of Isabella had been. Her mistress looked blank, and remained dumb–her master muttered something which sounded very like an oath–and poor Kate was so chop-fallen, she looked like a convicted criminal, who would gladly have hid herself, (now that the baseness was out,) to conceal her mortified pride and deep chagrin.

It was a fine triumph for Isabella and her master, and she became more ambitious than ever to please him; and he stimulated her ambition by his commendation, and by boasting of her to his friends, telling them that 'that wench' (pointing to Isabel) 'is better to me than a man–for she will do a good family's washing in the night, and be ready in the morning to go into the field, where she will do as much at raking and binding as my best hands.' Her ambition and desire to please were so great, that she often worked several nights in succession, sleeping only short snatches, as she sat in her chair; and some nights she would not allow herself to take any sleep, save what she could get resting herself against the wall, fearing that if she sat down, she would sleep too long. These extra exertions to please, and the praises consequent upon them, brought upon her head the envy of her fellow-slaves, and they taunted her with being the 'white folks' nigger.' On the other hand, she received the larger share of the confidence of her master, and many small favors that were by them unattainable. I asked her if her master, Dumont, ever whipped her? She answered, 'Oh yes, he some-times whipped me soundly, though never cruelly. And the most severe whipping he ever give me was because I was cruel to a cat.' At this time she looked upon her master as a God; and believed that he knew of and could see her at all times, even as God himself. And she used sometimes to confess her delinquencies, from the conviction that he already knew them, and that she should fare better if she confessed voluntarily: and if any one talked to her of the injustice of her being a slave, she answered them with contempt, and immediately told her master. She then firmly believed that slavery was right and honorable. Yet she now sees very clearly the false position they were all in, both masters and slaves; and she looks back, with utter astonishment, at the absurdity of the claims so arrogantly set up by the masters, over beings designed by God to be as free as kings; and at the perfect stupidity of the slave, in admitting for one moment the validity of these claims.

In obedience to her mother's instructions, she had educated her-self to such a sense of honesty, that, when she had become a mother, she would sometimes whip her child when it cried to her for bread, rather than give it a piece secretly, lest it should learn to take what was not its own! And the writer of this knows, from personal observation, that the slaveholders of the South feel it to be a religious duty to teach their slaves to be honest, and never to take what is not their own! Oh consistency, art thou not a jewel? Yet Isabella glories in the fact that she was faithful and true to her master; she says, 'It made me true to my God'–meaning, that it helped to form in her a character that loved truth, and hated a lie, and had saved her from the bitter pains and fears that are sure to follow in the wake of insincerity and hypocrisy.

As she advanced in years, an attachment sprung up between herself and a slave named Robert. But his master, an Englishman by the name of Catlin, anxious that no one's property but his own should be enhanced by the increase of his slaves, forbade Robert's visits to Isabella, and commanded him to take a wife among his fellow-servants. Notwithstanding this interdiction, Robert, following the bent of his inclinations, continued his visits to Isabel, though very stealthily, and, as he believed, without exciting the suspicion of his master; but one Saturday afternoon, hearing that Bell was ill, he took the liberty to go and see her. The first intimation she had of his visit was the appearance of her master, inquiring 'if she had seen Bob.' On her answering in the negative, he said to her, 'If you see him, tell him to take care of himself, for the Catlins are after him.' Almost at that instant, Bob made his appearance; and the first people he met were his old and his young masters. They were terribly enraged at finding him there, and the eldest began cursing, and calling upon his son to 'Knock down the d–d black rascal'; at the same time, they both fell upon him like tigers, beating him with the heavy ends of their canes, bruising and mangling his head and face in the most awful manner, and causing the blood, which streamed from his wounds, to cover him like a slaughtered beast, constituting him a most shocking spectacle. Mr. Dumont interposed at this point, telling the ruffians they could no longer thus spill human blood on his premises–he would have 'no niggers killed there.' The Catlins then took a rope they had taken with them for the purpose, and tied Bob's hands behind him in such a manner, that Mr. Dumont insisted on loosening the cord, declaring that no brute should be tied in that manner, where he was. And as they led him away, like the greatest of criminals, the more humane Dumont followed them to their homes, as Robert's protector; and when he returned, he kindly went to Bell, as he called her, telling her he did not think they would strike him any more, as their wrath had greatly cooled before he left them. Isabella had witnessed this scene from her window, and was greatly shocked at the murderous treatment of poor Robert, whom she truly loved, and whose only crime, in the eye of his persecutors, was his affection for her. This beating, and we know not what after treatment, completely subdued the spirit of its victim, for Robert ventured no more to visit Isabella, but like an obedient and faithful chattel, took himself a wife from the house of his master. Robert did not live many years after his last visit to Isabel, but took his departure to that country, where 'they neither marry nor are given in marriage,' and where the oppressor cannot molest.

ISABELLA'S MARRIAGE

Subsequently, Isabella was married to a fellow-slave, named Thomas, who had previously had two wives, one of whom, if not both, had been torn from him and sold far away. And it is more than probable, that he was not only allowed but encouraged to take another at each successive sale. I say it is probable, because the writer of this knows from personal observation, that such is the custom among slaveholders at the present day; and that in a twenty months' residence among them, we never knew any one to open the lip against the practice; and when we severely censured it, the slaveholder had nothing to say; and the slave pleaded that, under existing circumstances, he could do no better.

Such an abominable state of things is silently tolerated, to say the least, by slaveholders–deny it who may. And what is that religion that sanctions, even by its silence, all that is embraced in the 'Peculiar Institution? ' If there can be any thing more diametrically opposed to the religion of Jesus, than the working of this soul-killing system–which is as truly sanctioned by the religion of America as are her ministers and churches–we wish to be shown where it can be found.

We have said, Isabella was married to Thomas–she was, after the fashion of slavery, one of the slaves performing the ceremony for them; as no true minister of Christ can perform, as in the presence of God, what he knows to be a mere farce, a mock marriage, unrecognized by any civil law, and liable to be annulled any moment, when the interest or caprice of the master should dictate.

With what feelings must slaveholders expect us to listen to their horror of amalgamation in prospect, while they are well aware that we know how calmly and quietly they contemplate the present state of licentiousness their own wicked laws have created, not only as it regards the slave, but as it regards the more privileged portion of the population of the South?

Slaveholders appear to me to take the same notice of the vices of the slave, as one does of the vicious disposition of his horse. They are often an inconvenience; further than that, they care not to trouble themselves about the matter.

ISABELLA AS A MOTHER

In process of time, Isabella found herself the mother of five children, and she rejoiced in being permitted to be the instrument of increasing the property of her oppressors! Think, dear reader, without a blush, if you can, for one moment, of a mother thus willingly, and with pride, laying her own children, the 'flesh of her flesh,' on the altar of slavery–a sacrifice to the bloody Moloch! But we must remember that beings capable of such sacrifices are not mothers; they are only 'things,' 'chattels,' 'property.'

But since that time, the subject of this narrative has made some advances from a state of chattelism towards that of a woman and a mother; and she now looks back upon her thoughts and feelings there, in her state of ignorance and degradation, as one does on the dark imagery of a fitful dream. One moment it seems but a frightful illusion; again it appears a terrible reality. I would to God it were but a dreamy myth, and not, as it now stands, a horrid reality to some three millions of chattelized human beings.

I have already alluded to her care not to teach her children to steal, by her example; and she says, with groanings that cannot be written, 'The Lord only knows how many times I let my children go hungry, rather than take secretly the bread I liked not to ask for.' All parents who annul their preceptive teachings by their daily practices would do well to profit by her example.

Another proof of her master's kindness of heart is found in the following fact. If her master came into the house and found her infant crying, (as she could not always attend to its wants and the commands of her mistress at the same time,) he would turn to his wife with a look of reproof, and ask her why she did not see the child taken care of; saying, most earnestly, 'I will not hear this crying; I can't bear it, and I will not hear any child cry so. Here, Bell, take care of this child, if no more work is done for a week.' And he would linger to see if his orders were obeyed, and not countermanded.

When Isabella went to the field to work, she used to put her infant in a basket, tying a rope to each handle, and suspending the basket to a branch of a tree, set another small child to swing it. It was thus secure from reptiles and was easily administered to, and even lulled to sleep, by a child too young for other labors. I was quite struck with the ingenuity of such a baby-tender, as I have sometimes been with the swinging hammock the native mother prepares for her sick infant– apparently so much easier than aught we have in our more civilized homes; easier for the child, because it gets the motion without the least jar; and easier for the nurse, because the hammock is strung so high as to supersede the necessity of stooping.

SLAVEHOLDER'S PROMISES

After emancipation had been decreed by the State, some years before the time fixed for its consummation, Isabella's master told her if she would do well, and be faithful, he would give her 'free papers,' one year before she was legally free by statute. In the year 1826, she had a badly diseased hand, which greatly diminished her usefulness; but on the arrival of July 4, 1827, the time specified for her receiving her 'free papers,' she claimed the fulfillment of her master's promise; but he refused granting it, on account (as he alleged) of the loss he had sustained by her hand. She plead that she had worked all the time, and done many things she was not wholly able to do, although she knew she had been less useful than formerly; but her master remained inflexible. Her very faithfulness probably operated against her now, and he found it less easy than he thought to give up the profits of his faithful Bell, who had so long done him efficient service.

But Isabella inwardly determined that she would remain quietly with him only until she had spun his wool—about one hundred pounds—and then she would leave him, taking the rest of the time to herself. 'Ah!' she says, with emphasis that cannot be written, 'the slaveholders are TERRIBLE for promising to give you this or that, or such and such a privilege, if you will do thus and so; and when the time of fulfillment comes, and one claims the promise, they, forsooth, recollect nothing of the kind: and you are, like as not, taunted with being a LIAR; or, at best, the slave is accused of not having performed his part or condition of the contract.' 'Oh!' said she, 'I have felt as if I could not live through the operation sometimes. Just think of us! so eager for our pleasures, and just foolish enough to keep feeding and feeding ourselves up with the idea that we should get what had been thus fairly promised; and when we think it is almost in our hands, find ourselves flatly denied! Just think! how could we bear it? Why, there was Charles Brodhead promised his slave Ned, that when harvesting was over, he might go and see his wife, who lived some twenty or thirty miles off. So Ned worked early and late, and as soon as the harvest was all in, he claimed the promised boon. His master said, he had merely told him he 'would see if he could go, when the harvest was over; but now he saw that he could not go.' But Ned, who still claimed a positive promise, on which he had fully depended, went on cleaning his shoes. His master asked him if he intended going, and on his replying 'yes,' took up a sled-stick that lay near him, and gave him such a blow on the head as broke his skull, killing him dead on the spot. The poor colored people all felt struck down by the blow.' Ah! and well they might. Yet it was but one of a long series of bloody, and other most effectual blows, struck against their liberty and their lives.***** But to return from our digression.

The subject of this narrative was to have been free July 4, 1827, but she continued with her master till the wool was spun, and the heaviest of the 'fall's work' closed up, when she concluded to take her freedom into her own hands, and seek her fortune in some other place.

HER ESCAPE

The question in her mind, and one not easily solved, now was, 'How can I get away?' So, as was her usual custom, she 'told God she was afraid to go in the night, and in the day every body would see her.' At length, the thought came to her that she could leave just before the day dawned, and get out of the neighborhood where she was known before the people were much astir. 'Yes,' said she, fervently, 'that's a good thought! Thank you, God, for that thought!' So, receiving it as coming direct from God, she acted upon it, and one fine morning, a little before day-break, she might have been seen stepping stealthily away from the rear of Master Dumont's house, her infant on one arm and her wardrobe on the other; the bulk and weight of which, probably, she never found so convenient as on the present occasion, a cotton handkerchief containing both her clothes and her provisions.

As she gained the summit of a high hill, a considerable distance from her master's, the sun offended her by coming forth in all his pristine splendor. She thought it never was so light before; indeed, she thought it much too light. She sped to look about her, and ascertain if her pursuers were yet in sight. No one appeared, and, for the first time, the question came up for settlement, 'Where, and to whom, shall I go?' In all her thoughts of getting away, she had not once asked herself whither she should direct her steps. She sat down, fed her infant, and again turning her thoughts to God, her only help, she prayed him to direct her to some safe asylum. And soon it occurred to her, that there was a man living somewhere in the direction she had been pursuing, by the name of Levi Rowe, whom she had known, and who, she thought, would be likely to befriend her. She accordingly pursued her way to his house, where she found him ready to entertain and assist her, though he was then on his death-bed. He bade her partake of the hospitalities of his house, said he knew of two good places where she might get in, and requested his wife to show her where they were to be

---

***** Yet no official notice was taken of his more than brutal murder.

found. As soon as she came in sight of the first house, she recollected having seen it and its inhabitants before, and instantly exclaimed, 'That's the place for me; I shall s there.' She went there, and found the good people of the house, Mr. and Mrs. Van Wagener, absent, but was kindly received and hospitably entertained by their excellent mother, till the return of her children. When they arrived, she made her case known to them. They listened to her story, assuring her they never turned the needy away, and willingly gave her employment.

She had not been there long before her old master, Dumont, appeared, as she had anticipated; for when she took French leave of him, she resolved not to go too far from him, and not put him to as much trouble in looking her up–for the latter he was sure to do–as Tom and Jack had done when they ran away from him, a short time before. This was very considerate in her, to say the least, and a proof that 'like begets like.' He had often considered her feelings, though not always, and she was equally considerate.

When her master saw her, he said, 'Well, Bell, so you've run away from me.' 'No, I did not run away; I walked away by day-light, and all because you had promised me a year of my time.' His reply was, 'You must go back with me.' Her decisive answer was, 'No, I won't go back with you.' He said, 'Well, I shall take the child.' This also was as stoutly negatived.

Mr. Isaac S. Van Wagener then interposed, saying, he had never been in the practice of buying and selling slaves; he did not believe in slavery; but, rather than have Isabella taken back by force, he would buy her services for the balance of the year–for which her master charged twenty dollars, and five in addition for the child. The sum was paid, and her master Dumont departed; but not till he had heard Mr. Van Wagener tell her not to call him master–adding, 'there is but one master; and he who is your master is my master.' Isabella inquired what she should call him? He answered, 'call me Isaac Van Wagener, and my wife is Maria Van Wagener.' Isabella could not understand this, and thought it a mighty change, as it most truly was from a master whose word was law, to simple Isaac S. Van Wagener, who was master to no one. With these noble people, who, though they could not be the masters of slaves, were undoubtedly a portion of God's nobility, she resided one year, and from them she derived the name of Van Wagener; he being her last master in the eye of the law, and a slave's surname is ever the same as his master; that is, if he is allowed to have any other name than Tom, Jack, or Guffin. Slaves have sometimes been severely punished for adding their master's name to their own. But when they have no particular title to it, it is no particular offence.

ILLEGAL SALE OF HER SON

A little previous to Isabel's leaving her old master, he had sold her child, a boy of five years, to a Dr. Gedney, who took him with him as far as New York city, on his way to England; but finding the boy too small for his service, he sent him back to his brother, Solomon Gedney. This man disposed of him to his sister's husband, a wealthy planter, by the name of Fowler, who took him to his own home in Alabama.

This illegal and fraudulent transaction had been perpetrated some months before Isabella knew of it, as she was now living at Mr. Van Wagener's. The law expressly prohibited the sale of any slave out of the State,–and all minors were to be free at twenty-one years of age; and Mr. Dumont had sold Peter with the express understanding, that he was soon to return to the State of New York, and be emancipated at the specified time.

When Isabel heard that her son had been sold South, she immediately started on foot and alone, to find the man who had thus dared, in the face of all law, human and divine, to sell her child out of the State; and if possible, to bring him to account for the deed.

Arriving at New Paltz, she went directly to her former mistress, Dumont, complaining bitterly of the removal of her son. Her mistress heard her through, and then replied–'Ugh! a fine fuss to make about a little nigger! Why, haven't you as many of 'em left as you can see to, and take care of? A pity 'tis, the niggers are not all in Guinea!! Making such a halloo-balloo about the neighborhood; and all for a paltry nigger!!!' Isabella heard her through, and after a moment's hesitation, answered, in tones of deep determination–'I'll have my child again.' 'Have your child again!' repeated her mistress–her tones big with contempt, and scorning the absurd idea of her getting him. 'How can you get him? And what have you to support him with, if you could? Have you any money?' 'No,' answered Bell, 'I have no money, but God has enough, or what's better! And I'll have my child again.' These words were pronounced in the most slow, solemn, and determined measure and manner. And in speaking of it, she says, 'Oh my God! I know'd I'd have him agin. I was sure God would help me to get him. Why, I felt so tall within–I felt as if the power of a nation was with me!'

The impressions made by Isabella on her auditors, when moved by lofty or deep feeling, can never be transmitted to paper, (to use the words of another,) till by some Daguerrian act, we are enabled to transfer the look, the gesture, the tones of voice, in connection with the quaint, yet fit expressions used, and the spirit-stirring animation that, at such a time, pervades all she says.

After leaving her mistress, she called on Mrs. Gedney, mother of him who had sold her boy; who, after listening to her lamentations, her grief being mingled with indignation at the sale of her son, and her declaration that she would have him again—said, 'Dear me! What a disturbance to make about your child! What, is your child, better than my child? My child is gone out there, and yours is gone to live with her, to have enough of every thing, and be treated like a gentleman!' And here she laughed at Isabel's absurd fears, as she would represent them to be. 'Yes,' said Isabel, 'your child has gone there, but she is married, and my boy has gone as a slave, and he is too little to go so far from his mother. Oh, I must have my child.' And here the continued laugh of Mrs. G. seemed to Isabel, in this time of anguish and distress, almost demoniacal. And well it was for Mrs. Gedney, that, at that time, she could not even dream of the awful fate awaiting her own beloved daughter, at the hands of him whom she had chosen as worthy the wealth of her love and confidence, and in whose society her young heart had calculated on a happiness, purer and more elevated than was ever conferred by a kingly crown. But, alas! she was doomed to disappointment, as we shall relate by and by. At this point, Isabella earnestly begged of God that he would show to those about her that He was her helper; and she adds, in narrating, 'And He did; or, if He did not show them, he did me.'

IT IS OFTEN DARKEST JUST BEFORE DAWN

This homely proverb was illustrated in the case of our sufferer; for, at the period at which we have arrived in our narrative, to her the darkness seemed palpable, and the waters of affliction covered her soul; yet light was about to break in upon her.

Soon after the scenes related in our last chapter, which had harrowed up her very soul to agony, she met a man, (we would like to tell you who, dear reader, but it would be doing him no kindness, even at the present day, to do so,) who evidently sympathized with her, and counseled her to go to the Quakers, telling her they were already feeling very indignant at the fraudulent sale of her son, and assuring her that they would readily assist her, and direct her what to do. He pointed out to her two houses, where lived some of those people, who formerly, more than any other sect, perhaps, lived out the principles of the gospel of Christ. She wended her way to their dwellings, was listened to, unknown as she personally was to them, with patience, and soon gained their sympathies and active co-operation.

They gave her lodgings for the night; and it is very amusing to hear her tell of the 'nice, high, clean, white, beautiful bed' assigned her to sleep in, which contrasted so strangely with her former pallets, that she sat down and contemplated it, perfectly absorbed in wonder that such a bed should have been appropriated to one like herself. For some time she thought that she would lie down beneath it, on her usual bedstead, the floor. 'I did, indeed,' says she, laughing heartily at her former self. However, she finally concluded to make use of the bed, for fear that not to do so might injure the feelings of her good hostess. In the morning, the Quaker saw that she was taken and set down near Kingston, with directions to go to the Court House, and enter complaint to the Grand Jury.

By a little inquiry, she found which was the building she sought, went into the door, and taking the first man she saw of imposing appearance for the grand jury, she commenced her complaint. But he very civilly informed her there was no Grand Jury there; she must go up stairs. When she had with some difficulty ascended the flight through the crowd that filled them, she again turned to the 'grandest ' looking man she could select, telling him she had come to enter a complaint to the Grand Jury. For his own amusement, he inquired what her complaint was; but, when he saw it was a serious matter, he said to her, 'This is no place to enter a complaint–go in there,' pointing in a particular direction.

She then went in, where she found the Grand Jurors indeed sitting, and again commenced to relate her injuries. After holding some conversation among themselves, one of them rose, and bidding her follow him, led the way to a side office, where he heard her story, and asked her 'if she could swear that the child she spoke of was her son?' 'Yes,' she answered, 'I swear it's my son.' 'S, s!' said the lawyer, 'you must swear by this book'–giving her a book, which she thinks must have been the Bible. She took it, and putting it to her lips, began again to swear it was her child. The clerks, unable to preserve their gravity any longer, burst into an uproarious laugh; and one of them inquired of lawyer Chip of what use it could be to make her swear. 'It will answer the law,' replied the officer. He then made her comprehend just what he wished her to do, and she took a lawful oath, as far as the outward ceremony could make it one. All can judge how far she understood its spirit and meaning.

He now gave her a writ, directing her to take it to the constable at New Paltz, and have him serve it on Solomon Gedney. She obeyed, walking, or rather trotting, in her haste, some eight or nine miles.

But while the constable, through mistake, served the writ on a brother of the real culprit, Solomon Gedney slipped into a boat, and was nearly across the North River, on whose banks they were standing, before the dull Dutch constable was aware of his mistake. Solomon Gedney, meanwhile, consulted a lawyer, who advised him to go to Alabama and bring back the boy, otherwise it might cost him fourteen years' imprisonment, and a thousand dollars in cash. By this time, it is hoped he began to feel that selling slaves unlawfully was not so good a business as he had wished to find it. He secreted himself till due preparations could be made, and soon set sail for Alabama. Steamboats and railroads had not then annihilated distance to the extent they now have, and although he left in the fall of the year, spring came ere he returned, bringing the boy with him—but holding on to him as his property. It had ever been Isabella's prayer, not only that her son might be returned, but that he should be delivered from bondage, and into her own hands, lest he should be punished out of mere spite to her, who was so greatly annoying and irritating to her oppressors; and if her suit was gained, her very triumph would add vastly to their irritation.

She again sought advice of Esquire Chip, whose counsel was, that the aforesaid constable serve the before-mentioned writ upon the right person. This being done, soon brought Solomon Gedney up to Kingston, where he gave bonds for his appearance at court, in the sum of $600.

Esquire Chip next informed his client, that her case must now lie over till the next session of the court, some months in the future. 'The law must take its course,' said he.

'What! wait another court! wait months?' said the persevering mother. 'Why, long before that time, he can go clear off, and take my child with him—no one knows where. I cannot wait; I must have him now, whilst he is to be had.' 'Well,' said the lawyer, very coolly, 'if he puts the boy out of the way, he must pay the $600—one half of which will be yours'; supposing, perhaps, that $300 would pay for a 'heap of children,' in the eye of a slave who never, in all her life, called a dollar her own. But in this instance, he was mistaken in his reckoning. She assured him, that she had not been seeking money, neither would money satisfy her; it was her son, and her son alone she wanted, and her son she must have. Neither could she wait court, not she. The lawyer used his every argument to convince her, that she ought to be very thankful for what they had done for her; that it was a great deal, and it was but reasonable that she should now wait patiently the time of the court.

Yet she never felt, for a moment, like being influenced by these suggestions. She felt confident she was to receive a full and literal answer to her prayer, the burden of which had been–'O Lord, give my son into my hands, and that speedily! Let not the spoilers have him any longer.' Notwithstanding, she very distinctly saw that those who had thus far helped her on so kindly were wearied of her, and she feared God was wearied also. She had a short time previous learned that Jesus was a Saviour, and an intercessor; and she thought that if Jesus could but be induced to plead for her in the present trial, God would listen to him, though he were wearied of her importunities. To him, of course, she applied. As she was walking about, scarcely knowing whither she went, asking within herself, 'Who will show me any good, and lend a helping hand in this matter,' she was accosted by a perfect stranger, and one whose name she has never learned, in the following terms: 'Halloo, there; how do you get along with your boy? do they give him up to you?' She told him all, adding that now every body was tired, and she had none to help her. He said, 'Look here! I'll tell you what you'd better do. Do you see that stone house yonder?' pointing in a particular direction. 'Well, lawyer Demain lives there, and do you go to him, and lay your case before him; I think he'll help you. Stick to him. Don't give him peace till he does. I feel sure if you press him, he'll do it for you.' She needed no further urging, but trotted off at her peculiar gait in the direction of his house, as fast as possible,–and she was not encumbered with stockings, shoes, or any other heavy article of dress. When she had told him her story, in her impassioned manner, he looked at her a few moments, as if to ascertain if he were contemplating a new variety of the genus homo, and then told her, if she would give him five dollars, he would get her son for her, in twenty-four hours. 'Why,' she replied, 'I have no money, and never had a dollar in my life!' Said he, 'If you will go to those Quakers in Poppletown, who carried you to court, they will help you to five dollars in cash, I have no doubt; and you shall have your son in twenty-four hours, from the time you bring me that sum.' She performed the journey to Poppletown, a distance of some ten miles, very expeditiously; collected considerable more than the sum specified by the barrister; then, shutting the money tightly in her hand, she trotted back, and paid the lawyer a larger fee than he had demanded. When inquired of by people what she had done with the overplus, she answered, 'Oh, I got it for lawyer Demain, and I gave it to him. ' They assured her she was a fool to do so; that she should have kept all over five dollars, and purchased herself shoes with it. 'Oh, I do not want money or clothes now, I only want my son; and if five dollars will get him, more will surely get him. ' And if the lawyer had returned it to her, she avers she would not have accepted it. She was perfectly willing he should have every coin she could raise, if he would but restore her lost son to her. Moreover, the five dollars he required were for the remuneration of him who should go after her son and his master, and not for his own services.

The lawyer now renewed his promise, that she should have her son in twenty-four hours. But Isabella, having no idea of this space of time, went several times in a day, to ascertain if her son had come. Once, when the servant opened the door and saw her, she said, in a tone expressive of much surprise, 'Why, this woman's come again!' She then wondered if she went too often. When the lawyer appeared, he told her the twenty-four hours would not expire till the next morning; if she would call then, she would see her son. The next morning saw Isabel at the lawyer's door, while he was yet in his bed. He now assured her it was morning till noon; and that before noon her son would be there, for he had sent the famous 'Matty Styles' after him, who would not fail to have the boy and his master on hand in due season, either dead or alive; of that he was sure. Telling her she need not come again; he would himself inform her of their arrival.

After dinner, he appeared at Mr. Rutzer's, (a place the lawyer had procured for her, while she awaited the arrival of her boy,) assuring her, her son had come; but that he stoutly denied having any mother, or any relatives in that place; and said, 'she must go over and identify him.' She went to the office, but at sight of her the boy cried aloud, and regarded her as some terrible being, who was about to take him away from a kind and loving friend. He knelt, even, and begged them, with tears, not to take him away from his dear master, who had brought him from the dreadful South, and been so kind to him.

When he was questioned relative to the bad scar on his forehead, he said, 'Fowler's horse hove him.' And of the one on his cheek, 'That was done by running against the carriage.' In answering these questions, he looked imploringly at his master, as much as to say, 'If they are falsehoods, you bade me say them; may they be satisfactory to you, at least.'

78

The justice, noting his appearance, bade him forget his master and attend only to him. But the boy persisted in denying his mother, and clinging to his master, saying his mother did not live in such a place as that. However, they allowed the mother to identify her son; and Esquire Demain pleaded that he claimed the boy for her, on the ground that he had been sold out of the State, contrary to the laws in such cases made and provided–spoke of the penalties annexed to said crime, and of the sum of money the delinquent was to pay, in case any one chose to prosecute him for the offence he had committed. Isabella, who was sitting in a corner, scarcely daring to breathe, thought within herself, 'If I can but get the boy, the $200 may remain for whoever else chooses to prosecute–I have done enough to make myself enemies already'–and she trembled at the thought of the formidable enemies she had probably arrayed against herself–helpless and despised as she was. When the pleading was at an end, Isabella understood the Judge to declare, as the sentence of the Court, that the 'boy be delivered into the hands of the mother–having no other master, no other controller, no other conductor, but his mother.' This sentence was obeyed; he was delivered into her hands, the boy meanwhile begging, most piteously, not to be taken from his dear master, saying she was not his mother, and that his mother did not live in such a place as that. And it was some time before lawyer Demain, the clerks, and Isabella, could collectively succeed in calming the child's fears, and in convincing him that Isabella was not some terrible monster, as he had for the last months, probably, been trained to believe; and who, in taking him away from his master, was taking him from all good, and consigning him to all evil.

When at last kind words and bon-bons had quieted his fears, and he could listen to their explanations, he said to Isabella– 'Well, you do look like my mother used to'; and she was soon able to make him comprehend some of the obligations he was under, and the relation he stood in, both to herself and his master. She commenced as soon as practicable to examine the boy, and found, to her utter astonishment, that from the crown of his head to the sole of his foot, the callosities and indurations on his entire body were most frightful to behold. His back she described as being like her fingers, as she laid them side by side.

'Heavens! what is all this? ' said Isabel. He answered, 'It is where Fowler whipped, kicked, and beat me.' She exclaimed, 'Oh, Lord Jesus, look! see my poor child! Oh Lord, "render unto them double" for all this! Oh my God! Pete, how did you bear it?'

'Oh, this is nothing, mammy–if you should see Phillis, I guess you'd scare! She had a little baby, and Fowler cut her till the milk as well as blood ran down her body. You would scare to see Phillis, mammy.'

When Isabella inquired, 'What did Miss Eliza[†††††] say, Pete, when you were treated so badly?' he replied, 'Oh, mammy, she said she wished I was with Bell. Sometimes I crawled under the stoop, mammy, the blood running all about me, and my back would stick to the boards; and sometimes Miss Eliza would come and grease my sores, when all were abed and asleep.'

DEATH OF MRS. ELIZA FOWLER

As soon as possible she procured a place for Peter, as tender of locks, at a place called Wahkendall, near Greenkills. After he was thus disposed of, she visited her sister Sophia, who resided at Newberg, and spent the winter in several different families where she was acquainted. She remained some time in the family of a Mr. Latin, who was a relative of Solomon Gedney; and the latter, when he found Isabel with his cousin, used all his influence to persuade him she was a great mischief-maker and a very troublesome person,–that she had put him to some hundreds of dollars expense, by fabricating lies about him, and especially his sister and her family, concerning her boy, when the latter was living so like a gentleman with them; and, for his part, he would not advise his friends to harbor or encourage her. However, his cousins, the Latins, could not see with the eyes of his feelings, and consequently his words fell powerless on them, and they retained her in their service as long as they had aught for her to do. She then went to visit her former master, Dumont. She had scarcely arrived there, when Mr. Fred. Waring entered, and seeing Isabel, pleasantly accosted her, and asked her 'what she was driving at now-a-days.' On her answering 'nothing particular,' he requested her to go over to his place, and assist his folks, as some of them were sick, and they needed an extra hand. She very gladly assented. When Mr. W. retired, her master wanted to know why she wished to help people, that called her the 'worst of devils,' as Mr. Waring had done in the courthouse–for he was the uncle of Solomon Gedney, and attended the trial we have described–and declared 'that she was a fool to; he wouldn't do it.' 'Oh,' she told him, 'she would not mind that, but was very

---

[†††††] Meaning Mrs. Eliza Fowler.

glad to have people forget their anger towards her.' She went over, but too happy to feel that their resentment was passed, and commenced her work with a light heart and a strong will. She had not worked long in this frame of mind, before a young daughter of Mr. Waring rushed into the rooms exclaiming, with uplifted hands–'Heavens and earth, Isabella! Fowler's murdered Cousin Eliza!' 'Ho,' said Isabel, 'that's nothing–he liked to have killed my child; nothing saved him but God.' Meaning, that she was not at all surprised at it, for a man whose heart was sufficiently hardened to treat a mere child as hers had been treated, was, in her opinion, more fiend than human, and prepared for the commission of any crime that his passions might prompt him to. The child further informed her that a letter had arrived by mail bringing the news.

Immediately after this announcement, Solomon Gedney and his mother came in, going direct to Mrs. Waring's room, where she soon heard tones as of some one reading. She thought something said to her inwardly, 'Go up stairs and hear.' At first she hesitated, but it seemed to press her the more–'Go up and hear!' She went up, unusual as it is for slaves to leave their work and enter unbidden their mistress's room, for the sole purpose of seeing or hearing what may be seen or heard there. But on this occasion, Isabella says, she walked in at the door, shut it, placed her back against it, and listened. She saw them and heard them read–'He knocked her down with his fist, jumped on her with his knees, broke her collar-bone, and tore out her wind-pipe! He then attempted his escape, but was pursued and arrested, and put in an iron bank for safe-keeping!' And the friends were requested to go down and take away the poor innocent children who had thus been made in one short day more than orphans.

If this narrative should ever meet the eye of those innocent sufferers for another's guilt, let them not be too deeply affected by the relation; but, placing their confidence in Him who sees the end from the beginning, and controls the results, rest secure in the faith, that, although they may physically suffer for the sins of others, if they remain but true to themselves, their highest and more enduring interests can never suffer from such a cause. This relation should be suppressed for their sakes, were it not even now so often denied, that slavery is fast undermining all true regard for human life. We know this one instance is not a demonstration to the contrary; but, adding this to the lists of tragedies that weekly come up to us through the Southern mails, may we not admit them as proofs irrefragable? The newspapers confirmed this account of the terrible affair.

81

When Isabella had heard the letter, all being too much absorbed in their own feelings to take note of her, she returned to her work, her heart swelling with conflicting emotions. She was awed at the dreadful deed; she mourned the fate of the loved Eliza, who had in such an undeserved and barbarous manner been put away from her labors and watchings as a tender mother; and, 'last though not least,' in the development of her character and spirit, her heart bled for the afflicted relatives; even those of them who 'laughed at her calamity, and mocked when her fear came.' Her thoughts dwelt long and intently on the subject, and the wonderful chain of events that had conspired to bring her that day to that house, to listen to that piece of intelligence–to that house, where she never was before or afterwards in her life, and invited there by people who had so lately been hotly incensed against her. It all seemed very remarkable to her, and she viewed it as flowing from a special providence of God. She thought she saw clearly, that their unnatural bereavement was a blow dealt in retributive justice; but she found it not in her heart to exult or rejoice over them. She felt as if God had more than answered her petition, when she ejaculated, in her anguish of mind, 'Oh, Lord, render unto them double!' She said, 'I dared not find fault with God, exactly; but the language of my heart was, 'Oh, my God! that's too much–I did not mean quite so much, God!' It was a terrible blow to the friends of the deceased; and her selfish mother (who, said Isabella, made such a 'to-do about her boy, not from affection, but to have her own will and way') went deranged, and walking to and fro in her delirium, called aloud for her poor murdered daughter–'Eliza! Eliza! '

The derangement of Mrs. G. was a matter of hearsay, as Isabella saw her not after the trial; but she has no reason to doubt the truth of what she heard. Isabel could never learn the subsequent fate of Fowler, but heard, in the spring of '49, that his children had been seen in Kingston–one of whom was spoken of as a fine, interesting girl, albeit a halo of sadness fell like a veil about her.

ISABELLA'S RELIGIOUS EXPERIENCE

We will now turn from the outward and temporal to the inward and spiritual life of our subject. It is ever both interesting and instructive to trace the exercises of a human mind, through the trials and mysteries of life; and especially a naturally powerful mind, left as hers was almost entirely to its own workings, and the chance influences it met on its way; and especially to note its reception of that divine 'light, that lighteth every man that cometh into the world.'

We see, as knowledge dawns upon it, truth and error strangely commingled; here, a bright spot illuminated by truth–and there, one darkened and distorted by error; and the state of such a soul may be compared to a landscape at early dawn, where the sun is seen superbly gilding some objects, and causing others to send forth their lengthened, distorted, and sometimes hideous shadows.

Her mother, as we have already said, talked to her of God. From these conversations, her incipient mind drew the conclusion, that God was 'a great man'; greatly superior to other men in power; and being located 'high in the sky,' could see all that transpired on the earth. She believed he not only saw, but noted down all her actions in a great book, even as her master kept a record of whatever he wished not to forget. But she had no idea that God knew a thought of hers till she had uttered it aloud.

As we have before mentioned, she had ever been mindful of her mother's injunctions, spreading out in detail all her troubles before God, imploring and firmly trusting him to send her deliverance from them. Whilst yet a child, she listened to a story of a wounded soldier, left alone in the trail of a flying army, helpless and starving, who hardened the very ground about him with kneeling in his supplications to God for relief, until it arrived. From this narrative, she was deeply impressed with the idea, that if she also were to present her petitions under the open canopy of heaven, speaking very loud, she should the more readily be heard; consequently, she sought a fitting spot for this, her rural sanctuary. The place she selected, in which to offer up her daily orisons, was a small island in a small stream, covered with large willow shrubbery, beneath which the sheep had made their pleasant winding paths; and sheltering themselves from the scorching rays of a noon-tide sun, luxuriated in the cool shadows of the graceful willows, as they listened to the tiny falls of the silver waters. It was a lonely spot, and chosen by her for its beauty, its retirement, and because she thought that there, in the noise of those waters, she could speak louder to God, without being overheard by any who might pass that way. When she had made choice of her sanctum, at a point of the island where the stream met, after having been separated, she improved it by pulling away the branches of the shrubs from the centre, and weaving them together for a wall on the outside, forming a circular arched alcove, made entirely of the graceful willow. To this place she resorted daily, and in pressing times much more frequently.

At this time, her prayers, or, more appropriately, 'talks with God,' were perfectly original and unique, and would be well worth preserving, were it possible to give the tones and manner with the words; but no adequate idea of them can be written while the tones and manner remain inexpressible.

She would sometimes repeat, 'Our Father in heaven,' in her Low Dutch, as taught her by her mother; after that, all was from the suggestions of her own rude mind. She related to God, in minute detail, all her troubles and sufferings, inquiring, as she proceeded, 'Do you think that's right, God?' and closed by begging to be delivered from the evil, whatever it might be.

She talked to God as familiarly as if he had been a creature like herself; and a thousand times more so, than if she had been in the presence of some earthly potentate. She demanded, with little expenditure of reverence or fear, a supply of all her more pressing wants, and at times her demands approached very near to commands. She felt as if God was under obligation to her, much more than she was to him. He seemed to her benighted vision in some manner bound to do her bidding.

Her heart recoils now, with very dread, when she recalls those shocking, almost blasphemous conversations with great Jehovah. And well for herself did she deem it, that, unlike earthly potentates, his infinite character combined the tender father with the omniscient and omnipotent Creator of the universe.

She at first commenced promising God, that if he would help her out of all her difficulties, she would pay him by being very good; and this goodness she intended as a remuneration to God. She could think of no benefit that was to accrue to herself or her fellow-creatures, from her leading a life of purity and generous self-sacrifice for the good of others; as far as any but God was concerned, she saw nothing in it but heart-trying penance, sustained by the sternest exertion; and this she soon found much more easily promised than performed.

Days wore away–new trials came–God's aid was invoked, and the same promises repeated; and every successive night found her part of the contract unfulfilled. She now began to excuse herself, by telling God she could not be good in her present circumstances; but if he would give her a new place, and a good master and mistress, she could and would be good; and she expressly stipulated, that she would be good one day to show God how good she would be all of the time, when he should surround her with the right influences, and she should be delivered from the temptations that then so sorely beset her. But, alas! when night came, and she became conscious that she had yielded to all her temptations, and entirely failed of keeping her word with

God, having prayed and promised one hour, and fallen into the sins of anger and profanity the next, the mortifying reflection weighed on her mind, and blunted her enjoyment. Still, she did not lay it deeply to heart, but continued to repeat her demands for aid, and her promises of pay, with full purpose of heart, at each particular time, that that day she would not fail to keep her plighted word.

Thus perished the inward spark, like a flame just igniting, when one waits to see whether it will burn on or die out, till the long desired change came, and she found herself in a new place, with a good mistress, and one who never instigated an otherwise kind master to be unkind to her; in short, a place where she had literally nothing to complain of, and where, for a time, she was more happy than she could well express. 'Oh, every thing there was so pleasant, and kind, and good, and all so comfortable; enough of every thing; indeed, it was beautiful!' she exclaimed.

Here, at Mr. Van Wagener's,–as the reader will readily perceive she must have been,–she was so happy and satisfied, that God was entirely forgotten. Why should her thoughts turn to him, who was only known to her as a help in trouble? She had no trouble now; her every prayer had been answered in every minute particular. She had been delivered from her persecutors and temptations, her youngest child had been given her, and the others she knew she had no means of sustaining if she had them with her, and was content to leave them behind. Their father, who was much older than Isabel, and who preferred serving his time out in slavery, to the trouble and dangers of the course she pursued, remained with and could keep an eye on them–though it is comparatively little that they can do for each other while they remain in slavery; and this little the slave, like persons in every other situation of life, is not always disposed to perform. There are slaves, who, copying the selfishness of their superiors in power, in their conduct towards their fellows who may be thrown upon their mercy, by infirmity or illness, allow them to suffer for want of that kindness and care which it is fully in their power to render them.

The slaves in this country have ever been allowed to celebrate the principal, if not some of the lesser festivals observed by the Catholics and Church of England;–many of them not being required to do the least service for several days, and at Christmas they have almost universally an entire week to themselves, except, perhaps, the attending to a few duties, which are absolutely required for the comfort of the families they belong to. If much service is desired, they are hired to do it, and paid for it as if they were free. The more sober portion of them spend these holidays in earning a little money. Most of them visit and attend parties and balls, and not a few of them spend it in the lowest dissipation. This respite from toil is granted them by all religionists, of whatever persuasion, and probably originated from the fact that many of the first slaveholders were members of the Church of England.

Frederick Douglass, who has devoted his great heart and noble talents entirely to the furtherance of the cause of his down-trodden race, has said–'From what I know of the effect of their holidays upon the slave, I believe them to be among the most effective means, in the hands of the slaveholder, in keeping down the spirit of insurrection. Were the slaveholders at once to abandon this practice, I have not the slightest doubt it would lead to an immediate insurrection among the slaves. These holidays serve as conductors, or safety-valves, to carry off the rebellious spirit of enslaved humanity. But for these, the slave would be forced up to the wildest desperation; and woe betide the slaveholder, the day he ventures to remove or hinder the operation of those conductors! I warn him that, in such an event, a spirit will go forth in their midst, more to be dreaded than the most appalling earthquake.'

When Isabella had been at Mr. Van Wagener's a few months, she saw in prospect one of the festivals approaching. She knows it by none but the Dutch name, Pingster, as she calls it–but I think it must have been Whitsuntide, in English. She says she 'looked back into Egypt,' and every thing looked 'so pleasant there,' as she saw retrospectively all her former companions enjoying their freedom for at least a little space, as well as their wonted convivialities, and in her heart she longed to be with them. With this picture before her mind's eye, she contrasted the quiet, peaceful life she was living with the excellent people of Wahkendall, and it seemed so dull and void of incident, that the very contrast served but to heighten her desire to return, that, at least, she might enjoy with them, once more, the coming festivities. These feelings had occupied a secret corner of her breast for some time, when, one morning, she told Mrs. Van Wagener that her old master Dumont would come that day, and that she should go home with him on his return. They expressed some surprise, and asked her where she obtained her information. She replied, that no one had told her, but she felt that he would come.

It seemed to have been one of those 'events that cast their shadows before'; for, before night, Mr. Dumont made his appearance. She informed him of her intention to accompany him home. He answered, with a smile, 'I shall not take you back again; you ran away from me.' Thinking his manner contradicted his words, she did not feel repulsed, but made herself and child ready; and when her former master had seated himself in the open dearborn, she walked towards it, intending to place herself and child in the rear, and go with him. But, ere she reached the vehicle, she says that God revealed himself to her, with all the suddenness of a flash of lightning, showing her, 'in the twinkling of an eye, that he was all over'–that he pervaded the universe–'and that there was no place where God was not.' She became instantly conscious of her great sin in forgetting her almighty Friend and 'everpresent help in time of trouble.' All her unfulfilled promises arose before her, like a vexed sea whose waves run mountains high; and her soul, which seemed but one mass of lies, shrunk back aghast from the 'awful look' of him whom she had formerly talked to, as if he had been a being like herself; and she would now fain have hid herself in the bowels of the earth, to have escaped his dread presence. But she plainly saw there was no place, not even in hell, where he was not; and where could she flee? Another such 'a look,' as she expressed it, and she felt that she must be extinguished forever, even as one, with the breath of his mouth, 'blows out a lamp,' so that no spark remains.

A dire dread of annihilation now seized her, and she waited to see if, by 'another look,' she was to be stricken from existence,– swallowed up, even as the fire licketh up the oil with which it comes in contact.

When at last the second look came not, and her attention was once more called to outward things, she observed her master had left, and exclaiming aloud, 'Oh, God, I did not know you were so big,' walked into the house, and made an effort to resume her work. But the workings of the inward man were too absorbing to admit of much attention to her avocations. She desired to talk to God, but her vileness utterly forbade it, and she was not able to prefer a petition. 'What!' said she, 'shall I lie again to God? I have told him nothing but lies; and shall I speak again, and tell another lie to God?' She could not; and now she began to wish for some one to speak to God for her. Then a space seemed opening between her and God, and she felt that if some one, who was worthy in the sight of heaven, would but plead for her in their own name, and not let God know it came from her, who was so unworthy, God might grant it. At length a friend appeared to stand between herself and an insulted Deity; and she felt as sensibly refreshed as when, on a hot day, an umbrella had been interposed between her scorching head and a burning sun. But who was this friend? became the next inquiry. Was it Deencia, who had so often befriended her? She looked at her, with her new power of sight–and, lo! she, too, seemed all 'bruises and putrefying sores,' like herself. No, it was some one very different from Deencia.

'Who are you?' she exclaimed, as the vision brightened into a form distinct, beaming with the beauty of holiness, and radiant with love. She then said, audibly addressing the mysterious visitant–'I know you, and I don't know you.' Meaning, 'You seem perfectly familiar; I feel that you not only love me, but that you always have loved me–yet I know you not–I cannot call you by name.' When she said, 'I know you,' the subject of the vision remained distinct and quiet. When she said, 'I don't know you,' it moved restlessly about, like agitated waters. So while she repeated, without intermission, 'I know you, I know you,' that the vision might remain–'Who are you?' was the cry of her heart, and her whole soul was in one deep prayer that this heavenly personage might be revealed to her, and remain with her. At length, after bending both soul and body with the intensity of this desire, till breath and strength seemed failing, and she could maintain her position no longer, an answer came to her, saying distinctly, 'It is Jesus.' 'Yes,' she responded, 'it is Jesus.'

Previous to these exercises of mind, she heard Jesus mentioned in reading or speaking, but had received from what she heard no impression that he was any other than an eminent man, like a Washington or a Lafayette. Now he appeared to her delighted mental vision as so mild, so good, and so every way lovely, and he loved her so much! And, how strange that he had always loved her, and she had never known it! And how great a blessing he conferred, in that he should stand between her and God! And God was no longer a terror and a dread to her.

She sped not to argue the point, even in her own mind, whether he had reconciled her to God, or God to herself, (though she thinks the former now,) being but too happy that God was no longer to her as a consuming fire, and Jesus was 'altogether lovely.' Her heart was now full of joy and gladness, as it had been of terror, and at one time of despair. In the light of her great happiness, the world was clad in new beauty, the very air sparkled as with diamonds, and was redolent of heaven. She contemplated the unapproachable barriers that existed between herself and the great of this world, as the world calls greatness, and made surprising comparisons between them, and the union existing between herself and Jesus–Jesus, the transcendently lovely as well as great and powerful; for so he appeared to her, though he seemed but human; and she watched for his bodily appearance, feeling that she should know him, if she saw him; and when he came, she would go and dwell with him, as with a dear friend.

It was not given to her to see that he loved any other; and she thought if others came to know and love him, as she did, she should be thrust aside and forgotten, being herself but a poor ignorant slave, with little to recommend her to his notice. And when she heard him spoken off, she said mentally–'What! others know Jesus! I thought no one knew Jesus but me!' and she felt a sort of jealousy, lest she should be robbed of her newly found treasure.

She conceived, one day, as she listened to reading, that she heard an intimation that Jesus was married, and hastily inquired if Jesus had a wife. 'What!' said the reader, 'God have a wife?' 'Is Jesus God? ' inquired Isabella. 'Yes, to be sure he is,' was the answer returned. From this time, her conceptions of Jesus became more elevated and spiritual; and she sometimes spoke of him as God, in accordance with the teaching she had received.

But when she was simply told, that the Christian world was much divided on the subject of Christ's nature–some believing him to be coequal with the Father–to be God in and of himself, 'very God, of very God;'–some, that he is the 'well-beloved,' 'only begotten Son of God;'–and others, that he is, or was, rather, but a mere man–she said, 'Of that I only know as I saw. I did not see him to be God; else, how could he stand between me and God? I saw him as a friend, standing between me and God, through whom, love flowed as from a fountain.' Now, so far from expressing her views of Christ's character and office in accordance with any system of theology extant, she says she believes Jesus is the same spirit that was in our first parents, Adam and Eve, in the beginning, when they came from the hand of their Creator. When they sinned through disobedience, this pure spirit forsook them, and fled to heaven; that there it remained, until it returned again in the person of Jesus; and that, previous to a personal union with him, man is but a brute, possessing only the spirit of an animal.

She avers that, in her darkest hours, she had no fear of any worse hell than the one she then carried in her bosom; though it had ever been pictured to her in its deepest colors, and threatened her as a reward for all her misdemeanors. Her vileness and God's holiness and all-pervading presence, which filled immensity, and threatened her with constant annihilation, composed the burden of her vision of terror. Her faith in prayer is equal to her faith in the love of Jesus. Her language is, 'Let others say what they will of the efficacy of prayer, I

89

believe in it, and I shall pray. Thank God! Yes, I shall always pray,' she exclaims, putting her hands together with the greatest enthusiasm.

For some time subsequent to the happy change we have spoken off, Isabella's prayers partook largely of their former character; and while, in deep affliction, she labored for the recovery of her son, she prayed with constancy and fervor; and the following may be taken as a specimen:–'Oh, God, you know how much I am distressed, for I have told you again and again. Now, God, help me get my son. If you were in trouble, as I am, and I could help you, as you can me, think I wouldn't do it? Yes, God, you know I would do it.' 'Oh, God, you know I have no money, but you can make the people do for me, and you must make the people do for me. I will never give you peace till you do, God.' 'Oh, God, make the people hear me–don't let them turn me off, without hearing and helping me.' And she has not a particle of doubt, that God heard her, and especially disposed the hearts of thoughtless clerks, eminent lawyers, and grave judges and others– between whom and herself there seemed to her almost an infinite re- move–to listen to her suit with patient and respectful attention, backing it up with all needed aid. The sense of her nothingness in the eyes of those with whom she contended for her rights, sometimes fell on her like a heavy weight, which nothing but her unwavering confidence in an arm which she believed to be stronger than all others combined could have raised from her sinking spirit. 'Oh! how little did I feel,' she repeated, with a powerful emphasis. 'Neither would you wonder, if you could have seen me, in my ignorance and destitution, trotting about the streets, meanly clad, bare-headed, and bare-footed! Oh, God only could have made such people hear me; and he did it in answer to my prayers.' And this perfect trust, based on the rock of Deity, was a soul-protecting fortress, which, raising her above the battlements of fear, and shielding her from the machinations of the enemy, impelled her onward in the struggle, till the foe was vanquished, and the victory gained.

We have now seen Isabella, her youngest daughter, and her only son, in possession of, at least, their nominal freedom. It has been said that the freedom of the most free of the colored people of this country is but nominal; but stinted and limited as it is, at best, it is an immense remove from chattel slavery. This fact is disputed, I know; but I have no confidence in the honesty of such questionings. If they are made in sincerity, I honor not the judgment that thus decides.

Her husband, quite advanced in age, and infirm of health, was emancipated, with the balance of the adult slaves of the State, according to law, the following summer, July 4, 1828.

For a few years after this event, he was able to earn a scanty living, and when he failed to do that, he was dependent on the 'world's cold charity,' and died in a poorhouse. Isabella had herself and two children to provide for; her wages were trifling, for at that time the wages of females were at a small advance from nothing; and she doubtless had to learn the first elements of economy—for what slaves, that were never allowed to make any stipulations or calculations for themselves, ever possessed an adequate idea of the true value of time, or, in fact, of any material thing in the universe? To such, 'prudent using' is meanness—and 'saving' is a word to be sneered at. Of course, it was not in her power to make to herself a home, around whose sacred hearth-stone she could collect her family, as they gradually emerged from their prison-house of bondage; a home, where she could cultivate their affection, administer to their wants, and instill into the opening minds of her children those principles of virtue, and that love of purity, truth and benevolence, which must for ever form the foundation of a life of usefulness and happiness. No—all this was far beyond her power or means, in more senses than one; and it should be taken into the account, whenever a comparison is instituted between the progress made by her children in virtue and goodness, and the progress of those who have been nurtured in the genial warmth of a sunny home, where good influences cluster, and bad ones are carefully excluded—where 'line upon line, and precept upon precept,' are daily brought to their quotidian tasks—and where, in short, every appliance is brought in requisition, that self-denying parents can bring to bear on one of the dearest objects of a parent's life, the promotion of the welfare of their children. But God forbid that this suggestion should be wrested from its original intent, and made to shield any one from merited rebuke! Isabella's children are now of an age to know good from evil, and may easily inform themselves on any point where they may yet be in doubt; and if they now suffer themselves to be drawn by temptation into the paths of the destroyer, or forget what is due to the mother who has done and suffered so much for them, and who, now that she is descending into the vale of years, and feels her health and strength declining, will turn her expecting eyes to them for aid and comfort, just as instinctively as the child turns its confiding eye to its fond parent, when it seeks for succor or sympathy—(for it is now their turn to do the work, and bear the burdens of life, so all must bear them in turn, as the wheel of life rolls on)– if, I say, they forget this, their duty and their happiness, and pursue an opposite course of sin and folly, they must lose the respect of the wise and good, and find, when too late, that 'the way of the transgressor is hard.'

NEW TRIALS

The reader will pardon this passing homily, while we return to our narrative.

We were saying that the day-dreams of Isabella and her husband–the plan they drew of what they would do, and the comforts they thought to have, when they should obtain their freedom, and a little home of their own– had all turned to 'thin air,' by the postponement of their freedom to so late a day. These delusive hopes were never to be realized, and a new set of trials was gradually to open before her. These were the heart-wasting trials of watching over her children, scattered, and imminently exposed to the temptations of the adversary, with few, if any, fixed principles to sustain them.

'Oh,' she says, 'how little did I know myself of the best way to instruct and counsel them! Yet I did the best I then knew, when with them. I took them to the religious meetings; I talked to, and prayed for and with them; when they did wrong, I scolded at and whipped them.'

Isabella and her son had been free about a year, when they went to reside in the city of New York; a place which she would doubtless have avoided, could she have foreseen what was there in store for her; for this view into the future would have taught her what she only learned by bitter experience, that the baneful influences going up from such a city were not the best helps to education, commenced as the education of her children had been.

Her son Peter was, at the time of which we are speaking, just at that age when no lad should be subjected to the temptations of such a place, unprotected as he was, save by the feeble arm of a mother, herself a servant there. He was growing up to be a tall, well-formed, active lad, of quick perceptions, mild and cheerful in his disposition, with much that was open, generous and winning about him, but with little power to withstand temptation, and a ready ingenuity to provide himself with ways and means to carry out his plans, and conceal from his mother and her friends, all such as he knew would not meet their approbation. As will be readily believed, he was soon drawn into a circle of associates who did not improve either his habits or his morals.

Two years passed before Isabella knew what character Peter was establishing for himself among his low and worthless comrades–

passing under the assumed name of Peter Williams; and she began to feel a parent's pride in the promising appearance of her only son. But, alas! this pride and pleasure were shortly dissipated, as distressing facts relative to him came one by one to her astonished ear. A friend of Isabella's, a lady, who was much pleased with the good humor, inge- nuity, and open confessions of Peter, when driven into a corner, and who, she said, 'was so smart, he ought to have an education, if any one ought,'–paid ten dollars, as tuition fee, for him to attend a navigation school. But Peter, little inclined to spend his leisure hours in study, when he might be enjoying himself in the dance, or otherwise, with his boon companions, went regularly and made some plausible excuses to the teacher, who received them as genuine, along with the ten dollars of Mrs –, and while his mother and her friend believed him improving at school, he was, to their latent sorrow, improving in a very different place or places, and on entirely opposite principles. They also pro- cured him an excellent place as a coachman. But, wanting money, he sold his livery, and other things belonging to his master; who, having conceived a kind regard for him, considered his youth, and prevented the law from falling, with all its rigor, upon his head. Still he contin- ued to abuse his privileges, and to involve himself in repeated difficulties, from which his mother as often extricated him. At each time, she talked much, and reasoned and remonstrated with him; and he would, with such perfect frankness, lay open his whole soul to her, telling her he had never intended doing harm,–how he had been led along, little by little, till, before he was aware, he found himself in trouble–how he had tried to be good–and how, when he would have been so, 'evil was present with him,'–indeed he knew not how it was.

His mother, beginning to feel that the city was no place for him, urged his going to sea, and would have shipped him on board a man- of-war; but Peter was not disposed to consent to that proposition, while the city and its pleasures were accessible to him. Isabella now became a prey to distressing fears, dreading lest the next day or hour come fraught with the report of some dreadful crime, committed or abetted by her son. She thanks the Lord for sparing her that giant sor- row, as all his wrong doings never ranked higher, in the eye of the law, than misdemeanors. But as she could see no improvement in Peter, as a last resort, she resolved to leave him, for a time, unassisted, to bear the penalty of his conduct, and see what effect that would have on him. In the trial hour, she remained firm in her resolution. Peter again fell into the hands of the police, and sent for his mother, as usual; but she went not to his relief. In his extremity, he sent for Peter Williams, a respectable colored barber, whose name he had been wearing, and who sometimes helped young culprits out of their troubles, and sent them from city dangers, by shipping them on board of whaling vessels.

The curiosity of this man was awakened by the culprit's bearing his own name. He went to the Tombs and inquired into his case, but could not believe what Peter told him respecting his mother and family. Yet he redeemed him, and Peter promised to leave New York in a vessel that was to sail in the course of a week. He went to see his mother, and informed her of what had happened to him. She listened incredulously, as to an idle tale. He asked her to go with him and see for herself. She went, giving no credence to his story till she found herself in the presence of Mr. Williams, and heard him saying to her, 'I am very glad I have assisted your son; he stood in great need of sympathy and assistance; but I could not think he had such a mother here, although he assured me he had.'

Isabella's great trouble now was, a fear lest her son should deceive his benefactor, and be missing when the vessel sailed; but he begged her earnestly to trust him, for he said he had resolved to do better, and meant to abide by the resolve. Isabella's heart gave her no peace till the time of sailing, when Peter sent Mr. Williams and another messenger whom she knew, to tell her he had sailed. But for a month afterwards, she looked to see him emerging from some by-place in the city, and appearing before her; so afraid was she that he was still unfaithful, and doing wrong. But he did not appear, and at length she believed him really gone. He left in the summer of 1839, and his friends heard nothing further from him till his mother received the following letter, dated 'October 17 1840';-

MY DEAR AND BELOVED MOTHER:

'I take this opportunity to write to you and inform you that I am well, and in hopes for to find you the same. I am got on board the same unlucky ship Done, of Nantucket. I am sorry for to say, that I have been punished once severely, by shoving my head in the fire for other folks. We have had bad luck, but in hopes to have better. We have about 230 on board, but in hopes, if don't have good luck, that my parents will receive me with thanks. I would like to know how my sisters are. Does my cousins live in New York yet? Have you got my letter? If not, inquire to Mr. Pierce Whiting's. I wish you would write me an answer as soon as possible. I am your only son, that is so far from your home, in the wide briny ocean. I have seen more of the world than ever I expected, and if I ever should return home safe, I will tell you all my troubles and hardships. Mother, I hope you do not forget me, your dear and only son. I should like to know how Sophia, and Betsey, and Hannah, come on. I hope you all will forgive me for all that I have done. 'Your son, PETER VAN WAGENER.' Another letter reads as follows, dated 'March 22, 1841':-

'MY DEAR MOTHER: 'I take this opportunity to write to you, and inform you that I have been well and in good health. I have wrote you a letter before, but have received no answer from you, and was very anxious to see you. I hope to see you in a short time. I have had very hard luck, but are in hopes to have better in time to come. I should like if my sisters are well, and all the people round the neighborhood. I expect to be home in twenty-two months or thereabouts. I have seen Samuel Laterett. Beware! There has happened very bad news to tell you, that Peter Jackson is dead. He died within two days' sail of Otaheite, one of the Society Islands. The Peter Jackson that used to live at Laterett's; he died on board the ship Done, of Nantucket, Captain Miller, in the latitude 15 53, and longitude 148 30 W. I have no more to say at present, but write as soon as possible. 'Your only son, 'PETER VAN WAGENER.'

Another, containing the last intelligence she has had from her son, reads as follows, and was dated 'Sept. 19, 1841':-

'DEAR MOTHER:

'I take the opportunity to write to you and inform you that I am well and in good health, and in hopes to find you in the same. This is the fifth letter that I have wrote to you, and have received no answer, and it makes me very uneasy. So pray write as quick as you can, and tell me how all the people is about the neighborhood. We are out from home twenty-three months, and in hope to be home in fifteen months. I have not much to say; but tell me if you have been up home since I left or not. I want to know what sort of a time is at home. We had very bad luck when we first came out, but since we have had very good; so I am in hopes to do well yet; but if I don't do well, you need not expect me home these five years. So write as quick as you can, won't you? So now I am going to put an end to my writing, at present. Notice–when this you see, remember me, and place me in your mind.

Get me to my home, that's in the far distant west, To the scenes of my childhood, that I like the best; There the tall cedars grow, and the bright waters flow, Where my parents will greet me, white man, let me go! Let me go to the spot where the cataract plays, Where oft I have sported in my boyish days; And there is my poor mother, whose heart ever flows, At the sight of her poor child, to her let me go, let me go!

'Your only son,
'PETER VAN WAGENER.'

Since the date of the last letter, Isabella has heard no tidings from her long-absent son, though ardently does her mother's heart long for such tidings, as her thoughts follow him around the world, in his perilous vocation, saying within herself–'He is good now, I have no doubt; I feel sure that he has persevered, and kept the resolve he made before he left home;–he seemed so different before he went, so determined to do better.' His letters are inserted here for preservation, in case they prove the last she ever hears from him in this world.

FINDING A BROTHER AND SISTER

When Isabella had obtained the freedom of her son, she remained in Kingston, where she had been drawn by the judicial process, about a year, during which time she became a member of the Methodist Church there: and when she went to New York, she took a letter missive from that church to the Methodist Church in John street. Afterwards, she withdrew her connection with that church, and joined Zion's Church in Church street, composed entirely of colored people. With the latter church she remained until she went to reside with Mr. Pierson, after which, she was gradually drawn into the 'kingdom' set up by the prophet Matthias, in the name of God the Father; for he said the spirit of God the Father dwelt in him.

While Isabella was in New York, her sister Sophia came from Newburg to reside in the former place. Isabel had been favored with occasional interviews with this sister, although at one time she lost sight of her for the space of seventeen years–almost the entire period of her being at Mr. Dumont's–and when she appeared before her again, handsomely dressed, she did not recognize her, till informed who she was. Sophia informed her that her brother Michael–a brother she had never seen–was in the city; and when she introduced him to Isabella, he informed her that their sister Nancy had been living in the city, and had deceased a few months before. He described her features, her dress, her manner, and said she had for some time been a member in Zion's Church, naming the class she belonged to. Isabella almost instantly recognized her as a sister in the church, with whom she had knelt at the altar, and with whom she had exchanged the speaking pressure of the hand, in recognition of their spiritual sisterhood; little thinking, at the time, that they were also children of the same earthly parents–even Bomefree and Mau-mau Bett. As inquiries and answers rapidly passed, and the conviction deepened that this was their sister, the very sister they had heard so much of, but had never seen, (for she was the self-same sister that had been locked in the great old fashioned sleigh-box, when she was taken away, never to behold her mother's face again this side the spirit-land, and Michael, the narrator, was the brother who had shared her fate,) Isabella thought, 'D–h! here she was; we met; and was I not, at the time, struck with the peculiar feeling of her hand–the bony hardness so just like mine? and yet I could not know she was my sister; and now I see she looked so like my mother.' And Isabella wept, and not alone; Sophia wept, and the strong man, Michael, mingled his tears with theirs. 'Oh Lord,' inquired Isabella, 'what is this slavery, that it can do such dreadful things? what evil can it not do?' Well may she ask, for surely the evils it can and does do, daily and hourly, can never be summed up, till we can see them as they are recorded by him who writes no errors, and reckons without mistake. This account, which now varies so widely in the estimate of different minds, will be viewed alike by all.

Think you, dear reader, when that day comes, the most 'rapid abolitionist' will say–'Behold, I saw all this while on the earth?' Will he not rather say, 'Oh, who has conceived the breadth and depth of this moral malaria, this putrescent plague-spot?' Perhaps the pioneers in the slave's cause will be as much surprised as any to find that with all their looking, there remained so much unseen.

GLEANINGS

There are some hard things that crossed Isabella's life while in slavery, that she has no desire to publish, for various reasons. First, because the parties from whose hands she suffered them have rendered up their account to a higher tribunal, and their innocent friends alone are living, to have their feelings injured by the recital; secondly, because they are not all for the public ear, from their very nature; thirdly, and not least, because, she says, were she to tell all that happened to her as a slave–all that she knows is 'God's truth'–it would seem to others, especially the uninitiated, so unaccountable, so unreasonable, and what is usually called so unnatural, (though it may be questioned whether people do not always act naturally,) they would not easily believe it. 'Why, no!' she says, 'they'd call me a liar! they would, indeed! and I do not wish to say anything to destroy my own character for veracity, though what I say is strictly true.' Some things have been omitted through forgetfulness, which not having been mentioned in

their places, can only be briefly spoken of here;–such as, that her father Bomefree had had two wives before he took Mau-mau Bett; one
of whom, if not both, were torn from him by the iron hand of the ruth-
less trafficker in human flesh;–that her husband, Thomas, after one of
his wives had been sold away from him, ran away to New York City,
where he remained a year or two, before he was discovered and taken
back to the prison-house of slavery;–that her master Dumont, when he
promised Isabella one year of her time, before the State should make
her free, made the same promise to her husband, and in addition to
freedom, they were promised a log cabin for a home of their own; all
of which, with the one-thousand-and-one day-dreams resulting there-
from, went into the repository of unfulfilled promises and unrealized
hopes;–that she had often heard her father repeat a thrilling story of a
little slave-child, which, because it annoyed the family with its cries,
was caught up by a white man, who dashed its brains out against the
wall. An Indian (for Indians were plenty in that region then) passed
along as the bereaved mother washed the bloody corpse of her murdered child, and learning the cause of its death, said, with
characteristic vehemence, 'If I had been here, I would have put my
tomahawk in his head!' meaning the murderer's.

Of the cruelty of one Hasbrouck.–He had a sick slave-woman,
who was lingering with a slow consumption, whom he made to spin,
regardless of her weakness and suffering; and this woman had a child,
that was unable to walk or talk, at the age of five years, neither could it
cry like other children, but made a constant, piteous moaning sound.
This exhibition of helplessness and imbecility, instead of exciting the
master's pity, stung his cupidity, and so enraged him, that he would
kick the poor thing about like a foot-ball.

Isabella's informant had seen this brute of a man, when the child
was curled up under a chair, innocently amusing itself with a few
sticks, drag it hence, that he might have the pleasure of tormenting it.
She had see him, with one blow of his foot, send it rolling quite across
the room, and down the steps at the door. Oh, how she wished it might
instantly die! 'But,' she said, 'it seemed as tough as a moccasin.'
Though it did die at last, and made glad the heart of its friends; and its
persecutor, no doubt, rejoiced with them, but from very different motives. But the day of his retribution was not far off–for he sickened,
and his reason fled. It was fearful to hear his old slave soon tell how,
in the day of his calamity, she treated him.

She was very strong, and was therefore selected to support her
master, as he sat up in bed, by putting her arms around, while she

stood behind him. It was then that she did her best to wreak her vengeance on him. She would clutch his feeble frame in her iron grasp, as in a vice; and, when her mistress did not see, would give him a squeeze, a shake, and lifting him up, set him down again, as hard as possible. If his breathing betrayed too tight a grasp, and her mistress said, 'Be careful, don't hurt him, Soan!' her every-ready answer was, 'Oh no, Missus, no,' in her most pleasant tone–and then, as soon as Missus's eyes and ears were engaged away, another grasp–another shake–another bounce. She was afraid the disease alone would let him recover,–an event she dreaded more than to do wrong herself. Isabella asked her, if she were not afraid his spirit would haunt her. 'Oh, no,' says Soan; 'he was so wicked, the devil will never let him out of hell long enough for that.'

Many slaveholders boast of the love of their slaves. How would it freeze the blood of some of them to know what kind of love rankles in the bosoms of slaves for them! Witness the attempt to poison Mrs. Calhoun, and hundreds of similar cases. Most 'surprising ' to every body, because committed by slaves supposed to be so grateful for their chains.

These reflections bring to mind a discussion on this point, between the writer and a slaveholding friend in Kentucky, on Christmas morning, 1846. We had asserted, that until mankind were far in advance of what they are now, irresponsible power over our fellow-beings would be, as it is, abused. Our friend declared it was his conviction, that the cruelties of slavery existed chiefly in imagination, and that no person in D– County, where we then were, but would be above ill-treating a helpless slave. We answered, that if his belief was well-founded, the people in Kentucky were greatly in advance of the people of New England–for we would not dare say as much as that of any school-district there, letting alone counties. No, we would not answer for our own conduct even on so delicate a point.

The next evening, he very magnanimously overthrew his own position and established ours, by informing us that, on the morning previous, and as near as we could learn, at the very hour in which we were earnestly discussing the probabilities of the case, a young woman of fine appearance, and high standing in society, the pride of her husband, and the mother of an infant daughter, only a few miles from us, ay, in D– County, too, was actually beating in the skull of a slave-woman called Tabby; and not content with that, had her tied up and whipped, after her skull was broken, and she died hanging to the bedstead, to which she had been fastened. When informed that Tabby was

99

dead, she answered, 'I am glad of it, for she has worried my life out of me.' But Tabby's highest good was probably not the end proposed by Mrs. M–, for no one supposed she meant to kill her. Tabby was considered quite lacking in good sense, and no doubt belonged to that class at the South, that are silly enough to 'die of moderate correction.'

A mob collected around the house for an hour or two, in that manner expressing a momentary indignation. But was she treated as a murderess? Not at all! She was allowed to take boat (for her residence was near the beautiful Ohio) that evening, to spend a few months with her absent friends, after which she returned and remained with her husband, no one to 'molest or make her afraid.'

Had she been left to the punishment of an outraged conscience from right motives, I would have 'rejoiced with exceeding joy'. But to see the life of one woman, and she a murderess, put in the balance against the lives of three millions of innocent slaves, and to contrast her punishment with what I felt would be the punishment of one who was merely suspected of being an equal friend of all mankind, regardless of color or condition, caused my blood to stir within me, and my heart to sicken at the thought. The husband of Mrs. M– was absent from home, at the time alluded to; and when he arrived, some weeks afterwards, bringing beautiful presents to his cherished companion, he beheld his once happy home deserted, Tabby murdered and buried in the garden, and the wife of his bosom, and the mother of his child, the doer of a dreadful deed, a murderess!

When Isabella went to New York City, she went in company with a Miss Grear, who introduced her to the family of Mr. James Latourette, a wealthy merchant, and a Methodist in religion; but who, the latter part of his life, felt that he had outgrown ordinances, and advocated free meetings, holding them at his own dwelling-house for several years previous to his death. She worked for them, and they generously gave her a home while she labored for others, and in their kindness made her as one of their own.

At that time, the 'moral reform' movement was awakening the attention of the benevolent in that city. Many women, among whom were Mrs. Latourette and Miss Grear, became deeply interested in making an attempt to reform their fallen sisters, even the most degraded of them; and in this enterprise of labor and danger, they enlisted Isabella and others, who for a time put forth their most zealous efforts, and performed the work of missionaries with much apparent success. Isabella accompanied those ladies to the most wretched abodes of vice and misery, and sometimes she went where they dared not follow. They even succeeded in establishing prayer-meetings in several places, where such a thing might least have been expected.

But these meetings soon became the most noisy, shouting, ranting, and boisterous of gatherings; where they became delirious with excitement, and then exhausted from over-action. Such meetings Isabel had not much sympathy with, at best. But one evening she attended one of them, where the members of it, in a fit of ecstasy, jumped upon her cloak in such a manner as to drag her to the floor–and then, thinking she had fallen in a spiritual trance, they increased their glorifications on her account,–jumping, shouting, stamping, and clapping of hands; rejoicing so much over her spirit, and so entirely overlooking her body, that she suffered much, both from fear and bruises; and ever after refused to attend any more such meetings, doubting much whether God had any thing to do with such worship.

THE MATTHIAS DELUSION

We now come to an eventful period in the life of Isabella, as identified with one of the most extraordinary religious delusions of modern times; but the limits prescribed for the present work forbid a minute narration of all the occurrences that transpired in relation to it.

After she had joined the African Church in Church street, and during her membership there, she frequently attended Mr. Latourette's meetings, at one of which, Mr. Smith invited her to go to a prayer-meeting, or to instruct the girls at the Magdalene Asylum, Bowery Hill, then under the protection of Mr. Pierson, and some other persons, chiefly respectable females. To reach the Asylum, Isabella called on Katy, Mr. Pierson's colored servant, of whom she had some knowledge. Mr. Pierson saw her there, conversed with her, asked her if she had been baptized, and was answered, characteristically, 'by the Holy Ghost.' After this, Isabella saw Katy several times, and occasionally Mr. Pierson, who engaged her to keep his house while Katy went to Virginia to see her children. This engagement was considered an answer to a prayer by Mr. Pierson, who had both fasted and prayed on the subject, while Katy and Isabella appeared to see in it the hand of God.

Mr. Pierson was characterized by a strong devotional spirit, which finally became highly fanatical. He assumed the title of Prophet, asserting that God had called him in an omnibus, in these words:- 'Thou are Elijah, the Tishbite. Gather unto me all the members of Israel at the foot of Mount Carmel'; which he understood as meaning the gathering of his friends at Bowery Hill. Not long afterward, he became acquainted with the notorious Matthias, whose career was as extraordinary as it was brief. Robert Matthews, or Matthias (as he was usually called), was of Scotch extraction, but a native of Washington County, New York, and at that time about forty-seven years of age. He was religiously brought up, among the Anti-Burghers, a sect of Presbyterians; the clergyman, the Rev. Mr. Bevridge, visiting the family after the manner of the church, and being pleased with Robert, put his hand on his head, when a boy, and pronounced a blessing, and this blessing, with his natural qualities, determined his character; for he ever after thought he should be a distinguished man. Matthias was brought up a farmer till nearly eighteen years of age, but acquired indirectly the art of a carpenter, without any regular apprenticeship, and showed considerable mechanical skill. He obtained property from his uncle, Robert Thompson, and then he went into business as a store-keeper, was considered respectable, and became a member of the Scotch Presbyterian Church. He married in 1813, and continued in business in Cambridge. In 1816, he ruined himself by a building speculation, and the derangement of the currency which denied bank facilities, and soon after he came to New York with his family, and worked at his trade. He afterwards removed to Albany, and became a hearer at the Dutch Reformed Church, then under Dr. Ludlow's charge. He was frequently much excited on religious subjects.

In 1829, he was well known, if not for street preaching, for loud discussions and pavement exhortations, but he did not make set sermons. In the beginning of 1830, he was only considered zealous; but in the same year he prophesied the destruction of the Albanians and their capital, and while preparing to shave, with the Bible before him, he suddenly put down the soap and exclaimed, 'I have found it! I have found a text which proves that no man who shaves his beard can be a true Christian;' and shortly afterwards, without shaving, he went to the Mission House to deliver an address which he had promised, and in this address, he proclaimed his new character, pronounced vengeance on the land, and that the law of God was the only rule of government, and that he was commanded to take possession of the world in the name of the King of kings. His harangue was cut short by the trustees putting out the lights. About this time, Matthias laid by his implements of industry, and in June, he advised his wife to fly with him from the destruction which awaited them in the city; and on her refusal, partly on account of Matthias calling himself a Jew, whom she was unwilling to retain as a husband, he left her, taking some of the children to his sister in Argyle, forty miles from Albany. At Argyle he entered the church and interrupted the minister, declaring the congregation in darkness, and warning them to repentance. He was, of course, taken out of the church, and as he was advertised in the Albany papers, he was sent back to his family. His beard had now obtained a respectable length, and thus he attracted attention, and easily obtained an audience in the streets. For this he was sometimes arrested, once by mistake for Adam Paine, who collected the crowd, and then left Matthias with it on the approach of the officers. He repeatedly urged his wife to accompany him on a mission to convert the world, declaring that food could be obtained from the roots of the forest, if not administered otherwise. At this time he assumed the name of Matthias, called himself a Jew, and set out on a mission, taking a western course, and visiting a brother at Rochester, a skillful mechanic, since dead. Leaving his brother, he proceeded on his mission over the Northern States, occasionally returning to Albany.

After visiting Washington, and passing through Pennsylvania, he came to New York. His appearance at that time was mean, but grotesque, and his sentiments were but little known.

On May the 5th, 1832, he first called on Mr. Pierson, in Fourth street, in his absence. Isabella was alone in the house, in which she had lived since the previous autumn. On opening the door, she, for the first time, beheld Matthias, and her early impression of seeing Jesus in the flesh rushed to her mind. She heard his inquiry, and invited him into the parlor; and being naturally curious, and much excited, and possessing a good deal of tact, she drew him into conversation, stated her own opinions, and heard his replies and explanations. Her faith was at first staggered by his declaring himself a Jew; but on this point she was relieved by his saying, 'Do you not remember how Jesus prayed?' and repeated part of the Lord's Prayer, in proof that the Father's kingdom was to come, and not the Son's. She then understood him to be a converted Jew, and in the conclusion she says she 'felt as if God had sent him to set up the kingdom.' Thus Matthias at once secured the good will of Isabella, and we may supposed obtained from her some information in relation to Mr. Pierson, especially that Mrs. Pierson declared there was no true church, and approved of Mr. Pierson's preaching. Matthias left the house, promising to return on Saturday evening. Mr. P. at this time had not seen Matthias.

Isabella, desirous of hearing the expected conversation between Matthias and Mr. Pierson on Saturday, hurried her work, got it finished, and was permitted to be present. Indeed, the sameness of belief made her familiar with her employer, while her attention to her work,

and characteristic faithfulness, increased his confidence. This inti-
macy, the result of holding the same faith, and the principle afterwards
adopted of having but one table, and all things in common, made her at
once the domestic and the equal, and the depositary of very curious, if
not valuable information. To this object, even her color assisted. Persons who have traveled in the South know the manner in which the
colored people, and especially slaves, are treated; they are scarcely
regarded as being present. This trait in our American character has
been frequently noticed by foreign travelers. One English lady remarks
that she discovered, in course of conversation with a Southern married
gentleman, that a colored girl slept in his bedroom, in which also was
his wife; and when he saw that it occasioned some surprise, he remarked, 'What would he do if he wanted a glass of water in the night?'
Other travelers have remarked that the presence of colored people
never seemed to interrupt a conversation of any kind for one moment.
Isabella, then, was present at the first interview between Matthias and
Pierson. At this interview, Mr. Pierson asked Matthias if he had a family, to which he replied in the affirmative; he asked him about his
beard, and he gave a scriptural reason, asserting also that the Jews did
not shave, and that Adam had a beard. Mr. Pierson detailed to Matthias
his experience, and Matthias gave his, and they mutually discovered
that they held the same sentiments, both admitting the direct influence
of the Spirit, and the transmission of spirits from one body to another.
Matthias admitted the call of Mr. Pierson, in the omnibus in Wall
street, which, on this occasion, he gave in these words:–'Thou art
Elijah the Tishbite, and thou shalt go before me in the spirit and power
of Elias, to prepare my way before me.' And Mr. Pierson admitted
Matthias' call, who completed his declaration on the 20th of June, in
Argyle, which, by a curious coincidence, was the very day on which
Pierson had received his call in the omnibus. Such singular coinci-
dences have a powerful effect on excited minds. From that discovery,
Pierson and Matthias rejoiced in each other, and became kindred spirits–Matthias, however, claiming to be the Father, or to possess the
spirit of the Father–he was God upon the earth, because the spirit of
God dwelt in him; while Pierson then understood that his mission was
like that of John the Baptist, which the name Elias meant. This confer-
ence ended with an invitation to supper, and Matthias and Pierson
washing each other's feet. Mr. Pierson preached on the following Sunday, but after which, he declined in favor of Matthias, and some of the
party believed that the 'kingdom had then come.'

As a specimen of Matthias' preaching and sentiments, the following is said to be reliable:

'The spirit that built the Tower of Babel is now in the world–it is the spirit of the devil. The spirit of man never goes upon the clouds; all who think so are Babylonians. The only heaven is on earth. All who are ignorant of truth are Ninevites. The Jews did not crucify Christ– it was the Gentiles. Every Jew has his guardian angel attending him in this world. God don't speak through preachers; he speaks through me, his prophet. ' " John the Baptist," (addressing Mr. Pierson), "read the tenth chapter of Revelations."

After the reading of the chapter, the prophet resumed speaking, as follows:-

'Ours is the mustard-seed kingdom which is to spread all over the earth. Our creed is truth, and no man can find truth unless he obeys John the Baptist, and comes clean into the church. 'All real men will be saved; all mock men will be damned. When a person has the Holy Ghost, then he is a man, and not till then. They who teach women are of the wicked. The communion is all nonsense; so is prayer. Eating a nip of bread and drinking a little wine won't do any good. All who admit members into their church, and suffer them to hold their lands and houses, their sentence is, "Depart, ye wicked, I know you not." All females who lecture their husbands, their sentence is the same. The sons of truth are to enjoy all the good things of this world, and must use their means to bring it about. Every thing that has the smell of woman will be destroyed. Woman is the capsheaf of the abomination of desolation–full of all deviltry. In a short time, the world will take fire and dissolve; it is combustible already. All women, not obedient, had better become so as soon as possible, and let the wicked spirit depart, and become temples of truth. Praying is all mocking. When you see any one wring the neck of a fowl, instead of cutting off its head, he has not got the Holy Ghost. (Cutting gives the least pain.) 'All who eat swine's flesh are of the devil; and just as certain as he eats it, he will tell a lie in less than half an hour. If you eat a piece of pork, it will go crooked through you, and the Holy Ghost will not stay in you, but one or the other must leave the house pretty soon. The pork will be as crooked in you as ram's horns, and as great a nuisance as the hogs in the street. 'The cholera is not the right word; it is choler, which means God's wrath. Abraham, Isaac, and Jacob are now in this world; they did not go up in the clouds, as some believe–why should they go there? They don't want to go there to box the compass from one place to another. The Christians now-a-days are for setting up the Son's kingdom. It is not his; it is the Father's kingdom. It puts me in mind of a man in the country, who took his son in business, and had his sign made, "Hitchcock & Son;" but the son wanted it "Hitchcock & Father"–and that is the way with your Christians. They talk of the Son's kingdom first, and not the Father's kingdom.'

Matthias and his disciples at this time did not believe in a resurrection of the body, but that the spirits of the former saints would enter the bodies of the present generation, and thus begin heaven on earth, of which he and Mr. Pierson were the first fruits.

Matthias made the residence of Mr. Pierson his own; but the latter, being apprehensive of popular violence in his house, if Matthias remained there, proposed a monthly allowance to him, and advised him to occupy another dwelling. Matthias accordingly took a house in Clarkson street, and then sent for his family at Albany, but they declined coming to the city. However, his brother George complied with a similar offer, bringing his family with him, where they found very comfortable quarters. Isabella was employed to do the housework. In May, 1833, Matthias left his house, and placed the furniture, part of which was Isabella's, elsewhere, living himself at the hotel corner of Marketfield and West streets. Isabella found employment at Mr. Whiting's, Canal street, and did the washing for Matthias by Mrs. Whiting's permission.

Of the subsequent removal of Matthias to the farm and residence of Mr. B. Folger, at Sing Sing, where he was joined by Mr. Pierson, and others laboring under a similar religious delusion–the sudden, melancholy and somewhat suspicious death of Mr. Pierson, and the arrest of Matthias on the charge of his murder, ending in a verdict of not guilty–the criminal connection that subsisted between Matthias, Mrs. Folger, and other members of the 'Kingdom,' as 'match-spirits'- the final dispersion of this deluded company, and the voluntary exilement of Matthias in the far West, after his release–&c. &c., we do not deem it useful or necessary to give any particulars. Those who are curious to know what there transpired are referred to a work published in New York in 1835, entitled 'Fanaticism; its Sources and Influence; illustrated by the simple Narrative of Isabella, in the case of Matthias, Mr. and Mrs. B. Folger, Mr. Pierson, Mr. Mills, Catharine, Isabella, &c. &c. By G. Vale, 84 Roosevelt street.' Suffice it to say, that while Isabella was a member of the household at Sing Sing, doing much laborious service in the spirit of religious disinterestedness, and gradually getting her vision purged and her mind cured of its illusions, she happily escaped the contamination that surrounded her,–

assiduously endeavoring to discharge all her duties in a becoming manner.

FASTING

When Isabella resided with Mr. Pierson, he was in the habit of fasting every Friday; not eating or drinking anything from Thursday evening to six o'clock on Friday evening.

Then, again, he would fast two nights and three days, neither eating nor drinking; refusing himself even a cup of cold water till the third day at night, when he took supper again, as usual.

Isabella asked him why he fasted. He answered, that fasting gave him great light in the things of God; which answer gave birth to the following train of thought in the mind of his auditor:-'Well, if fasting will give light inwardly and spiritually, I need it as much as any body,–and I'll fast too. If Mr. Pierson needs to fast two nights and three days, then I, who need light more than he does, ought to fast more, and I will fast three nights and three days.'

This resolution she carried out to the letter, putting not so much as a drop of water in her mouth for three whole days and nights. The fourth morning, as she arose to her feet, not having the power to stand, she fell to the floor; but recovering herself sufficiently, she made her way to the pantry, and feeling herself quite voracious, and fearing that she might now offend God by her voracity, compelled herself to breakfast on dry bread and water–eating a large six-penny loaf before she felt at all stayed or satisfied. She says she did get light, but it was all in her body and none in her mind–and this lightness of body lasted a long time. Oh! she was so light, and felt so well, she could 'skim around like a gull.'

THE CAUSE OF HER LEAVING THE CITY

The first years spent by Isabella in the city, she accumulated more than enough to satisfy all her wants, and she placed all the overplus in the Savings' Bank. Afterwards, while living with Mr. Pierson, he prevailed on her to take it all thence, and invest it in a common fund which he was about establishing, as a fund to be drawn from by all the faithful; the faithful, of course, were the handful that should subscribe to his peculiar creed. This fund, commenced by Mr. Pierson, afterwards became part and parcel of the kingdom of which Matthias assumed to be head; and at the breaking up of the kingdom, her little property was merged in the general ruin–or went to enrich those who profited by the loss of others, if any such there were. Mr. Pierson and others had so assured her, that the fund would supply all her wants, at all times, and in all emergencies, and to the end of life, that she became perfectly careless on the subject–asking for no interest when she drew her money from the bank, and taking no account of the sum she placed in the fund. She recovered a few articles of the furniture from the wreck of the kingdom, and received a small sum of money from Mr. B. Folger, as the price of Mrs. Folger's attempt to convict her of murder. With this to start upon, she commenced anew her labors, in the hope of yet being able to accumulate a sufficiency to make a little home for herself, in her advancing age. With this stimulus before her, she toiled hard, working early and late, doing a great deal for a little money, and turning her hand to almost anything that promised good pay. Still, she did not prosper, and somehow, could not contrive to lay by a single dollar for a 'rainy day.'

When this had been the state of her affairs some time, she suddenly paused, and taking a retrospective view of what had passed, inquired within herself, why it was that, for all her unwearied labors, she had nothing to show; why it was that others, with much less care and labor, could hoard up treasures for themselves and children? She became more and more convinced, as she reasoned, that every thing she had undertaken in the city of New York had finally proved a failure; and where her hopes had been raised the highest, there she felt the failure had been the greatest, and the disappointment most severe.

After turning it in her mind for some time, she came to the conclusion, that she had been taking part in a great drama, which was, in itself, but one great system of robbery and wrong. 'Yes,' she said, 'the rich rob the poor, and the poor rob one another.' True, she had not received labor from others, and stinted their pay, as she felt had been practised against her; but she had taken their work from them, which was their only means to get money, and was the same to them in the end. For instance–a gentleman where she lived would give her a dollar to hire a poor man to clear the new-fallen snow from the steps and side-walks. She would arise early, and perform the labor herself, putting the money into her own pocket. A poor man would come along, saying she ought to have let him have the job; he was poor, and needed the pay for his family. She would harden her heart against him, and answer–'I am poor too, and I need it for mine.' But, in her retrospection, she thought of all the misery she might have been adding to, in her selfish grasping, and it troubled her conscience sorely; and this insensibility to the claims of human brotherhood, and the wants of the destitute and wretched poor, she now saw, as she never had done before, to be unfeeling, selfish and wicked. These reflections and convictions gave rise to a sudden revulsion of feeling in the heart of Isabella, and she began to look upon money and property with great indifference, if not contempt–being at that time unable, probably, to discern any difference between a miserly grasping at and hoarding of money and means, and a true use of the good things of this life for one's own comfort, and the relief of such as she might be enabled to befriend and assist. One thing she was sure of–that the precepts, 'Do unto others as ye would that others should do unto you,' 'Love your neighbor as yourself,' and so forth, were maxims that had been but little thought of by herself, or practised by those about her.

Her next decision was, that she must leave the city; it was no place for her; yea, she felt called in spirit to leave it, and to travel east and lecture. She had never been further east than the city, neither had she any friends there of whom she had particular reason to expect any thing; yet to her it was plain that her mission lay in the east, and that she would find friends there. She determined on leaving; but these determinations and convictions she kept close locked in her own breast, knowing that if her children and friends were aware of it, they would make such an ado about it as would render it very unpleasant, if not distressing to all parties. Having made what preparations for leaving she deemed necessary,–which was, to put up a few articles of clothing in a pillow-case, all else being deemed an unnecessary incumbrance,– about an hour before she left, she informed Mrs. Whiting, the woman of the house where she was staying, that her name was no longer Isabella, but SOJOURNER; and that she was going east. And to her inquiry, 'What are you going east for?' her answer was, 'The Spirit calls me there, and I must go.'

She left the city on the morning of the 1st of June, 1843, crossing over to Brooklyn, L.I.; and taking the rising sun for her only compass and guide, she 'remembered Lot's wife,' and hoping to avoid her fate, she resolved not to look back till she felt sure the wicked city from which she was fleeing was left too far behind to be visible in the distance; and when she first ventured to look back, she could just discern the blue cloud of smoke that hung over it, and she thanked the Lord that she was thus far removed from what seemed to her a second Sodom.

She was now fairly started on her pilgrimage; her bundle in one hand, and a little basket of provisions in the other, and two York shillings in her purse–her heart strong in the faith that her true work lay before her, and that the Lord was her director; and she doubted not he would provide for and protect her, and that it would be very censurable in her to burden herself with any thing more than a moderate supply for her then present needs. Her mission was not merely to travel east, but to 'lecture,' as she designated it; 'testifying of the hope that was in her'–exhorting the people to embrace Jesus, and refrain from sin, the nature and origin of which she explained to them in accordance with her own most curious and original views. Through her life, and all its chequered changes, she has ever clung fast to her first permanent impressions on religious subjects.

Wherever night overtook her, there she sought for lodgings–free, if she might–if not, she paid; at a tavern, if she chanced to be at one–if not, at a private dwelling; with the rich, if they would receive her–if not, with the poor.

But she soon discovered that the largest houses were nearly always full; if not quite full, company was soon expected; and that it was much easier to find an unoccupied corner in a small house than in a large one; and if a person possessed but a miserable roof over his head, you might be sure of a welcome to part of it.

But this, she had penetration enough to see, was quite as much the effect of a want of sympathy as of benevolence; and this was also very apparent in her religious conversations with people who were strangers to her. She said, 'she never could find out that the rich had any religion. If I had been rich and accomplished, I could; for the rich could always find religion in the rich, and I could find it among the poor.'

At first, she attended such meetings as she heard of, in the vicinity of her travels, and spoke to the people as she found them assembled. Afterwards, she advertised meetings of her own, and held forth to large audiences, having, as she said, 'a good time.'

When she became weary of travelling, and wished a place to s a while and rest herself, she said some opening for her was always near at hand; and the first time she needed rest, a man accosted her as she was walking, inquiring if she was looking for work. She told him that was not the object of her travels, but that she would willingly work a few days, if any one wanted. He requested her to go to his family, who were sadly in want of assistance, which he had been thus far unable to supply. She went to the house where she was directed, and was received by his family, one of whom was ill, as a 'Godsend;' and when she felt constrained to resume her journey, they were very sorry, and would fain have detained her longer; but as she urged the necessity of leaving, they offered her what seemed in her eyes a great deal of money as a remuneration for her labor, and an expression of their gratitude for her opportune assistance; but she would only receive a very little of it; enough, as she says, to enable her to pay tribute to Caesar, if it was demanded of her; and two or three York shillings at a time were all she allowed herself to take; and then, with purse replenished, and strength renewed, she would once more set out to perform her mission.

THE CONSEQUENCES OF REFUSING A TRAVELLER A NIGHT'S LODGING

As she drew near the center of the Island, she commenced, one evening at nightfall, to solicit the favor of a night's lodging. She had repeated her request a great many, it seemed to her some twenty times, and as many times she received a negative answer. She walked on, the stars and the tiny horns of the new moon shed but a dim light on her lonely way, when she was familiarly accosted by two Indians, who took her for an acquaintance. She told them they were mistaken in the person; she was a stranger there, and asked them the direction to a tavern. They informed her it was yet a long way–some two miles or so; and inquired if she were alone. Not wishing for their protection, or knowing what might be the character of their kindness, she answered, 'No, not exactly,' and passed on. At the end of a weary way, she came to the tavern,–or rather, to a large building, which was occupied as a court-house, tavern, and jail,–and on asking for a night's lodging, was informed she could stay, if she would consent to be locked in. This to her mind was an insuperable objection. To have a key turned on her was a thing not to be thought of, at least not to be endured, and she again took up her line of march, preferring to walk beneath the open sky, to being locked up by a stranger in such a place. She had not walked far, before she heard the voice of a woman under an open shed;

she ventured to accost her, and inquired if she knew where she could get in for the night. The woman answered, that she did not, unless she went home with them; and turning to her 'good man,' asked him if the stranger could not share their home for the night, to which he cheerfully assented. Sojourner thought it evident he had been taking a drop too much, but as he was civil and good-natured, and she did not feel inclined to spend the night alone in the open air, she felt driven to the necessity of accepting their hospitality, whatever it might prove to be. The woman soon informed her that there was a ball in the place, at which they would like to drop in a while, before they went to their home.

Balls being no part of Sojourner's mission, she was not desirous of attending; but her hostess could be satisfied with nothing short of a taste of it, and she was forced to go with her, or relinquish their company at once, in which move there might be more exposure than in accompanying her. She went, and soon found herself surrounded by an assemblage of people, collected from the very dregs of society, too ignorant and degraded to understand, much less entertain, a high or bright idea,–in a dirty hovel, destitute of every comfort, and where the fumes of whiskey were abundant and powerful.

Sojourner's guide there was too much charmed with the combined entertainments of the place to be able to tear herself away, till she found her faculties for enjoyment failing her, from a too free use of liquor; and she betook herself to bed till she could recover them. Sojourner, seated in a corner, had time for many reflections, and refrained from lecturing them, in obedience to the recommendation, 'Cast not your pearls,' &c. When the night was far spent, the husband of the sleeping woman aroused the sleeper, and reminded her that she was not very polite to the woman she had invited to sleep at her house, and of the propriety of returning home. They once more emerged into the pure air, which to our friend Sojourner, after so long breathing the noisome air of the ball-room, was most refreshing and grateful. Just as day dawned, they reached the place they called their home. Sojourner now saw that she had lost nothing in the shape of rest by remaining so long at the ball, as their miserable cabin afforded but one bunk or pallet for sleeping; and had there been many such, she would have preferred sitting up all night to occupying one like it. They very politely offered her the bed, if she would use it; but civilly declining, she waited for morning with an eagerness of desire she never felt before on the subject, and was never more happy than when the eye of day shed its golden light once more over the earth. She was once more free, and while daylight should last, independent, and needed no invitation to pursue her journey. Let these facts teach us, that every pedestrian in the world is not a vagabond, and that it is a dangerous thing to compel any one to receive that hospitality from the vicious and abandoned which they should have received from us,–as thousands can testify, who have thus been caught in the snares of the wicked.

The fourth of July, Isabella arrived at Huntingdon; from thence she went to Cold Springs, where she found the people making preparations for a mass temperance-meeting. With her usual alacrity, she entered into their labors, getting up dishes a la New York, greatly to the satisfaction of those she assisted. After remaining at Cold Springs some three weeks, she returned to Huntingdon, where she took boat for Connecticut. Landing at Bridgeport, she again resumed her travels towards the north-east, lecturing some, and working some, to get wherewith to pay tribute to Caesar, as she called it; and in this manner she presently came to the city of New Haven, where she found many meetings, which she attended–at some of which, she was allowed to express her views freely, and without reservation. She also called meetings expressly to give herself an opportunity to be heard; and found in the city many true friends of Jesus, as she judged, with whom she held communion of spirit, having no preference for one sect more than another, but being well satisfied with all who gave her evidence of having known or loved the Savior.

After thus delivering her testimony in this pleasant city, feeling she had not as yet found an abiding place, she went from thence to Bristol, at the request of a zealous sister, who desired her to go to the latter place, and hold a religious conversation with some friends of hers there. She went as requested, found the people kindly and religiously disposed, and through them she became acquainted with several very interesting persons.

A spiritually-minded brother in Bristol, becoming interested in her new views and original opinions, requested as a favor that she would go to Hartford, to see and converse with friends of his there. Standing ready to perform any service in the Lord, she went to Hartford as desired, bearing in her hand the following note from this brother:-

'SISTER,-I send you this living messenger, as I believe her to be one that God loves. Ethiopia is stretching forth her hands unto God. You can see by this sister, that God does by his Spirit alone teach his own children things to come. Please receive her, and she will tell you some new things. Let her tell her story without interrupting her, and give close attention, and you will see she has got the lever of truth, that God helps her to pry where but few can. She cannot read or write, but the law is in her heart. 'Send her to brother –, brother –, and where she can do the most good. 'From your brother, H. L. B.'

SOME OF HER VIEWS AND REASONINGS

As soon as Isabella saw God as an all-powerful, all-pervading spirit, she became desirous of hearing all that had been written of him, and listened to the account of the creation of the world and its first inhabitants, as contained in the first chapters of Genesis, with peculiar interest. For some time she received it all literally, though it appeared strange to her that 'God worked by the day, got tired, and sped to rest,' &c. But after a little time, she began to reason upon it, thus–'Why, if God works by the day, and one day's work tires him, and he is obliged to rest, either from weariness or on account of darkness, or if he waited for the "cool of the day to walk in the garden," because he was inconvenienced by the heat of the sun, why then it seems that God cannot do as much as I can; for I can bear the sun at noon, and work several days and nights in succession without being much tired. Or, if he rested nights because of the darkness, it is very queer that he should make the night so dark that he could not see himself. If I had been God, I would have made the night light enough for my own convenience, surely.' But the moment she placed this idea of God by the side of the impression she had once so suddenly received of his inconceivable greatness and entire spirituality, that moment she exclaimed mentally, 'No, God does not s to rest, for he is a spirit, and cannot tire; he cannot want for light, for he hath all light in himself. And if "God is all in all," and "worketh all in all," as I have heard them read, then it is impossible he should rest at all; for if he did, every other thing would s and rest too; the waters would not flow, and the fishes could not swim; and all motion must cease. God could have no pauses in his work, and he needed no Sabbaths of rest. Man might need them, and he should take them when he needed them, whenever he required rest. As it regarded the worship of God, he was to be worshipped at all times and in all places; and one portion of time never seemed to her more holy than another.'

These views, which were the results of the workings of her own mind, assisted solely by the light of her own experience and very limited knowledge, were, for a long time after their adoption, closely locked in her own breast, fearing lest their avowal might bring upon her the imputation of 'infidelity,'–the usual charge preferred by all religionists, against those who entertain religious views and feelings differing materially from their own. If, from their own sad experience, they are withheld from shouting the cry of 'infidel,' they fail not to see and to feel, ay, and to say, that the dissenters are not of the right spirit, and that their spiritual eyes have never been unsealed.

114

While travelling in Connecticut, she met a minister, with whom she held a long discussion on these points, as well as on various other topics, such as the origin of all things, especially the origin of evil, at the same time bearing her testimony strongly against a paid ministry. He belonged to that class, and, as a matter of course, as strongly advocated his own side of the question.

I had forgotten to mention, in its proper place, a very important fact, that when she was examining the Scriptures, she wished to hear them without comment; but if she employed adult persons to read them to her, and she asked them to read a passage over again, they invariably commenced to explain, by giving her their version of it; and in this way, they tried her feelings exceedingly.

In consequence of this, she ceased to ask adult persons to read the Bible to her, and substituted children in their stead. Children, as soon as they could read distinctly, would re-read the same sentence to her, as often as she wished, and without comment; and in that way she was enabled to see what her own mind could make out of the record, and that, she said, was what she wanted, and not what others thought it to mean. She wished to compare the teachings of the Bible with the witness within her; and she came to the conclusion, that the spirit of truth spoke in those records, but that the recorders of those truths had intermingled with them ideas and suppositions of their own. This is one among the many proofs of her energy and independence of character.

When it became known to her children, that Sojourner had left New York, they were filled with wonder and alarm. Where could she have gone, and why had she left? were questions no one could answer satisfactorily. Now, their imaginations painted her as a wandering maniac–and again they feared she had been left to commit suicide; and many were the tears they shed at the loss of her.

But when she reached Berlin, Conn., she wrote to them by amanuensis, informing them of her whereabouts, and waiting an answer to her letter; thus quieting their fears, and gladdening their hearts once more with assurances of her continued life and her love.

THE SECOND ADVENT DOCTRINES

In Hartford and vicinity, she met with several persons who believed in the 'Second Advent' doctrines; or, the immediate personal appearance of Jesus Christ. At first she thought she had never heard of 'Second Advent.' But when it was explained to her, she recollected having once attended Mr. Miller's meeting in New York, where she saw a great many enigmatical pictures hanging on the wall, which she could not understand, and which, being out of the reach of her understanding, failed to interest her. In this section of country, she attended two camp-meetings of the believers in these doctrines–the 'second advent' excitement being then at its greatest height. The last meeting was at Windsor Lock. The people, as a matter of course, eagerly inquired of her concerning her belief, as it regarded their most important tenet. She told them it had not been revealed to her; perhaps, if she could read, she might see it differently. Sometimes, to their eager inquiry, 'Oh, don't you believe the Lord is coming?' she answered, 'I believe the Lord is as near as he can be, and not be it.' With these evasive and non-exciting answers, she kept their minds calm as it respected her unbelief, till she could have an opportunity to hear their views fairly stated, in order to judge more understandingly of this matter, and see if, in her estimation, there was any good ground for expecting an event which was, in the minds of so many, as it were, shaking the very foundations of the universe. She was invited to join them in their religious exercises, and accepted the invitation–praying, and talking in her own peculiar style, and attracting many about her by her singing.

When she had convinced the people that she was a lover of God and his cause, and had gained a good standing with them, so that she could get a hearing among them, she had become quite sure in her own mind that they were laboring under a delusion, and she commenced to use her influence to calm the fears of the people, and pour oil upon the troubled waters. In one part of the grounds, she found a knot of people greatly excited: she mounted a stump and called out, 'Hear! hear!' When the people had gathered around her, as they were in a state to listen to any thing new, she addressed them as 'children,' and asked them why they made such a 'To-do;–are you not commanded to "watch and pray?" You are neither watching nor praying.' And she bade them, with the tones of a kind mother, retire to their tents, and there watch and pray, without noise or tumult, for the Lord would not come to such a scene of confusion; 'the Lord came still and quiet.' She assured them, 'the Lord might come, move all through the camp, and go away again, and they never know it,' in the state they then were.

They seemed glad to seize upon any reason for being less agitated and distressed, and many of them suppressed their noisy terror, and retired to their tents to 'watch and pray;' begging others to do the same, and listen to the advice of the good sister. She felt she had done some good, and then went to listen further to the preachers. They appeared to her to be doing their utmost to agitate and excite the people,

116

who were already too much excited; and when she had listened till her feelings would let her listen silently no longer, she arose and addressed the preachers. The following are specimens of her speech:-

'Here you are talking about being "changed in the twinkling of an eye." If the Lord should come, he'd change you to nothing! for there is nothing to you.

'You seem to be expecting to go to some parlor away up somewhere, and when the wicked have been burnt, you are coming back to walk in triumph over their ashes–this is to be your New Jerusalem!! Now, I can't see any thing so very nice in that, coming back to such a muss as that will be, a world covered with the ashes of the wicked! Besides, if the Lord comes and burns–as you say he will–I am not going away; I am going to stay here and stand the fire, like Shadrach, Meshach, and Abednego! And Jesus will walk with me through the fire, and keep me from harm. Nothing belonging to God can burn, any more than God himself; such shall have no need to go away to escape the fire! No, I shall remain. Do you tell me that God's children can't stand fire?' And her manner and tone spoke louder than words, saying, 'It is absurd to think so!'

The ministers were taken quite aback at so unexpected an opposer, and one of them, in the kindest possible manner, commenced a discussion with her, by asking her questions, and quoting scripture to her; concluding, finally, that although she had learned nothing of the great doctrine which was so exclusively occupying their minds at the time, she had learned much that man had never taught her.

At this meeting, she received the address of different persons, residing in various places, with an invitation to visit them. She promised to go soon to Cabotville, and started, shaping her course for that place. She arrived at Springfield one evening at six o'clock, and immediately began to search for a lodging for the night. She walked from six till past nine, and was then on the road from Springfield to Cabotville, before she found any one sufficiently hospitable to give her a night's shelter under their roof. Then a man gave her twenty-five cents, and bade her go to a tavern and stay all night. She did so, returning in the morning to thank him, assuring him she had put his money to its legitimate use. She found a number of the friends she had seen at Windsor when she reached the manufacturing town of Cabotville, (which has lately taken the name of Chicopee,) and with them she spent a pleasant week or more; after which, she left them to visit the Shaker village in Enfield. She now began to think of finding a resting place, at least, for a season; for she had performed quite a long journey, considering she had walked most of the way; and she had a mind to look in upon the Shakers, and see how things were there, and whether there was any opening there for her. But on her way back to Springfield, she called at a house and asked for a piece of bread; her request was granted, and she was kindly invited to tarry all night, as it was getting late, and she would not be able to stay at every house in that vicinity, which invitation she cheerfully accepted. When the man of the house came in, he recollected having seen her at the camp-meeting, and repeated some conversations, by which she recognized him again. He soon proposed having a meeting that evening, went out and notified his friends and neighbors, who came together, and she once more held forth to them in her peculiar style. Through the agency of this meeting, she became acquainted with several people residing in Springfield, to whose houses she was cordially invited, and with whom she spent some pleasant time.

One of these friends, writing of her arrival there, speaks as follows. After saying that she and her people belonged to that class of persons who believed in the second advent doctrines; and that this class, believing also in freedom of speech and action, often found at their meetings many singular people, who did not agree with them in their principal doctrine; and that, being thus prepared to hear new and strange things, 'They listened eagerly to Sojourner, and drank in all she said;'—and also, that she 'soon became a favorite among them; that when she arose to speak in their assemblies, her commanding figure and dignified manner hushed every trifler into silence, and her singular and sometimes uncouth modes of expression never provoked a laugh, but often were the whole audience melted into tears by her touching stories.' She also adds, 'Many were the lessons of wisdom and faith I have delighted to learn from her.' . . . . 'She continued a great favorite in our meetings, both on account of her remarkable gift in prayer, and still more remarkable talent for singing, . . . and the aptness and point of her remarks, frequently illustrated by figures the most original and expressive.

'As we were walking the other day, she said she had often thought what a beautiful world this would be, when we should see every thing right side up. Now, we see every thing topsy-turvy, and all is confusion.' For a person who knows nothing of this fact in the science of optics, this seemed quite a remarkable idea.

'We also loved her for her sincere and ardent piety, her unwavering faith in God, and her contempt of what the world calls fashion, and what we call folly. 'She was in search of a quiet place, where a way-worn traveler might rest. She had heard of Fruitlands, and was inclined to go there; but the friends she found here thought it best for her to visit Northampton. She passed her time, while with us, working wherever her work was needed, and talking where work was not needed. 'She would not receive money for her work, saying she worked for the Lord; and if her wants were supplied, she received it as from the Lord. 'She remained with us till far into winter, when we introduced her at the Northampton Association.' . . . . 'She wrote to me from thence, that she had found the quiet resting place she had so long desired. And she has remained there ever since.'

ANOTHER CAMP MEETING

When Sojourner had been at Northampton a few months, she attended another camp-meeting, at which she performed a very important part.

A party of wild young men, with no motive but that of entertaining themselves by annoying and injuring the feelings of others, had assembled at the meeting, hooting and yelling, and in various ways interrupting the services, and causing much disturbance. Those who had the charge of the meeting, having tried their persuasive powers in vain, grew impatient and tried threatening.

The young men, considering themselves insulted, collected their friends, to the number of a hundred or more, dispersed themselves through the grounds, making the most frightful noises, and threatening to fire the tents. It was said the authorities of the meeting sat in grave consultation, decided to have the ring-leaders arrested, and sent for the constable, to the great displeasure of some of the company, who were opposed to such an appeal to force and arms. Be that as it may, Sojourner, seeing great consternation depicted in every countenance, caught the contagion, and, ere she was aware, found herself quaking with fear.

Under the impulse of this sudden emotion, she fled to the most retired corner of a tent, and secreted herself behind a trunk. saying to herself, 'I am the only colored person here, and on me, probably, their wicked mischief will fall first, and perhaps fatally.' But feeling how great was her insecurity even there, as the very tent began to shake from its foundations, she began to soliloquize as follows:-

'Shall I run away and hide from the Devil? Me, a servant of the living God? Have I not faith enough to go out and quell that mob, when I know it is written–"One shall chase a thousand, and two put ten thousand to flight"? I know there are not a thousand here; and I know I am a servant of the living God. I'll go to the rescue, and the Lord shall go with and protect me. 'Oh,' said she, 'I felt as if I had three hearts! and that they were so large, my body could hardly hold them!'

She now came forth from her hiding-place, and invited several to go with her and see what they could do to still the raging of the moral elements. They declined, and considered her wild to think of it.

The meeting was in the open fields–the full moon shed its saddened light over all–and the woman who was that evening to address them was trembling on the preachers' stand. The noise and confusion were now terrific. Sojourner left the tent alone and unaided, and walking some thirty rods to the of a small rise of ground, commenced to sing, in her most fervid manner, with all the strength of her most powerful voice, the hymn on the resurrection of Christ–

It was early in the morning–it was early in the morning, Just at the break of day– When he rose–when he rose–when he rose, And went to heaven on a cloud.'

All who have ever heard her sing this hymn will probably remember it as long as they remember her. The hymn, the tune, the style, are each too closely associated with to be easily separated from herself, and when sung in one of her most animated moods, in the open air, with the utmost strength of her most powerful voice, must have been truly thrilling.

As she commenced to sing, the young men made a rush towards her, and she was immediately encircled by a dense body of the rioters, many of them armed with sticks or clubs as their weapons of defense, if not of attack. As the circle narrowed around her, she ceased singing, and after a short pause, inquired, in a gentle but firm tone, 'Why do you come about me with clubs and sticks? I am not doing harm to any one.' 'We ar'n't a going to hurt you, old woman; we came to hear you sing,' cried many voices, simultaneously. 'Sing to us, old woman,' cries one. 'Talk to us, old woman,' says another. 'Pray, old woman,' says a third. 'Tell us your experience,' says a fourth. 'You stand and smoke so near me, I cannot sing or talk,' she answered.

'Stand back,' said several authoritative voices, with not the most gentle or courteous accompaniments, raising their rude weapons in the air. The crowd suddenly gave back, the circle became larger, as many voices again called for singing, talking, or praying, backed by assurances that no one should be allowed to hurt her–the speakers declaring with an oath, that they would 'knock down ' any person who should offer her the least indignity.

She looked about her, and with her usual discrimination, said inwardly–'Here must be many young men in all this assemblage, bearing within them hearts susceptible of good impressions. I will speak to them.' She did speak; they silently heard, and civilly asked her many questions. It seemed to her to be given her at the time to answer them with truth and wisdom beyond herself. Her speech had operated on the roused passions of the mob like oil on agitated waters; they were, as a whole, entirely subdued, and only clamored when she ceased to speak or sing. Those who stood in the back ground, after the circle was enlarged, cried out, 'Sing aloud, old woman, we can't hear.' Those who held the scepter of power among them requested that she should make a pulpit of a neighboring wagon. She said, 'If I do, they'll overthrow it.' 'No, they can't–he who dares hurt you, we'll knock him down instantly, d–n him,' cried the chiefs. 'No we won't, no we won't, nobody shall hurt you,' answered the many voices of the mob. They kindly assisted her to mount the wagon, from which she spoke and sung to them about an hour. Of all she said to them on the occasion, she remembers only the following:-

'Well, there are two congregations on this ground. It is written that there shall be a separation, and the sheep shall be separated from the goats. The other preachers have the sheep, I have the goats. And I have a few sheep among my goats, but they are very ragged.' This exordium produced great laughter. When she became wearied with talking, she began to cast about her to contrive some way to induce them to disperse. While she paused, they loudly clamored for 'more,' 'more,'–'sing,' 'sing more.' She motioned them to be quiet, and called out to them: 'Children, I have talked and sung to you, as you asked me; and now I have a request to make of you; will you grant it?' 'Yes, yes, yes,' resounded from every quarter. 'Well, it is this,' she answered; 'if I will sing one more hymn for you, will you then go away, and leave us this night in peace?' 'Yes, yes,' came faintly, feebly from a few. 'I repeat it,' says Sojourner, 'and I want an answer from you all, as of one accord. If I will sing you one more, will you go away, and leave us this night in peace?' 'Yes, yes, yes,' shouted many voices, with hearty emphasis. 'I repeat my request once more,' said she, 'and I want you all to answer.' And she reiterated the words again. This time a long, loud 'Yes–yes–yes,' came up, as from the multitudinous mouth of the entire mob. 'AMEN! it is SEALED,' repeated Sojourner, in the deepest and most solemn tones of her powerful and sonorous voice. Its effect ran through the multitude, like an electric shock; and the most of them considered themselves bound by their promise, as they might have failed to do under less imposing circumstances. Some of them began instantly to leave; others said, 'Are we not to have one more hymn?' 'Yes,' answered their entertainer, and she commenced to sing:

'I bless the Lord I've got my seal–to-day and to-day– To slay Goliath in the field–to-day and to-day; The good old way is a righteous way, I mean to take the kingdom in the good old way.'

While singing, she heard some enforcing obedience to their promise, while a few seemed refusing to abide by it. But before she had quite concluded, she saw them turn from her, and in the course of a few minutes, they were running as fast as they well could in a solid body; and she says she can compare them to nothing but a swarm of bees, so dense was their phalanx, so straight their course, so hurried their march. As they passed with a rush very near the stand of the other preachers, the hearts of the people were smitten with fear, thinking that their entertainer had failed to enchain them longer with her spell, and that they were coming upon them with redoubled and remorseless fury. But they found they were mistaken, and that their fears were groundless; for, before they could well recover from their surprise, every rioter was gone, and not one was left on the grounds, or seen there again during the meeting. Sojourner was informed that as her audience reached the main road, some distance from the tents, a few of the rebellious spirits refused to go on, and proposed returning; but their leaders said, 'No–we have promised to leave–all promised, and we must go, all go, and you shall none of you return again.'

She did not fall in love at first sight with the Northampton Association, for she arrived there at a time when appearances did not correspond with the ideas of associationists, as they had been spread out in their writings; for their phalanx was a factory, and they were wanting in means to carry out their ideas of beauty and elegance, as they would have done in different circumstances. But she thought she would make an effort to tarry with them one night, though that seemed to her no desirable affair. But as soon as she saw that accomplished, literary, and refined persons were living in that plain and simple manner, and submitting to the labors and privations incident to such an infant institution, she said, 'Well, if these can live here, I can.' Afterwards, she gradually became pleased with, and attached to, the place and the people, as well she might; for it must have been no small thing to have found a home in a 'Community composed of some of the choicest spirits of the age,' where all was characterized by an equality of feeling, a liberty of thought and speech, and a largeness of soul, she could not have before met with, to the same extent, in any of her wanderings.

Our first knowledge of her was derived from a friend who had resided for a time in the 'Community,' and who, after describing her, and singing one of her hymns, wished that we might see her. But we little thought, at that time, that we should ever pen these 'simple annals' of this child of nature.

When we first saw her, she was working with a hearty good will; saying she would not be induced to take regular wages, believing, as once before, that now Providence had provided her with a never-failing fount, from which her every want might be perpetually supplied through her mortal life. In this, she had calculated too fast. For the Associationists found, that, taking every thing into consideration, they would find it most expedient to act individually; and again, the subject of this sketch found her dreams unreal, and herself flung back upon her own resources for the supply of her needs. This she might have found more inconvenient at her time of life–for labor, exposure, and hardship had made sad inroads upon her iron constitution, by inducing chronic disease and premature old age–had she not remained under the shadow of one,[‡‡‡‡‡] who never wearies in doing good, giving to the needy, and supplying the wants of the destitute. She has now set her heart upon having a little home of her own, even at this late hour of life, where she may feel a greater freedom than she can in the house of another, and where she can repose a little, after her day of action has passed by. And for such a 'home' she is now dependant on the charities of the benevolent, and to them we appeal with confidence.

Through all the scenes of her eventful life may be traced the energy of a naturally powerful mind–the fearlessness and child-like simplicity of one untrammeled by education or conventional customs– purity of character–an unflinching adherence to principle–and a native enthusiasm, which, under different circumstances, might easily have produced another Joan of Arc.

With all her fervor, and enthusiasm, and speculation, her religion is not tinctured in the least with gloom. No doubt, no hesitation, no despondency, spreads a cloud over her soul; but all is bright, clear, positive, and at times ecstatic. Her trust is in God, and from him she looks for good, and not evil. She feels that 'perfect love casteth out fear.'

[‡‡‡‡‡] GEORGE W. BENSON.

Having more than once found herself awaking from a mortifying delusion,–as in the case of the Sing-Sing kingdom,–and resolving not to be thus deluded again, she has set suspicion to guard the door of her heart, and allows it perhaps to be aroused by too slight causes, on certain subjects–her vivid imagination assisting to magnify the phantoms of her fears into gigantic proportions, much beyond their real size; instead of resolutely adhering to the rule we all like best, when it is to be applied to ourselves–that of placing every thing we see to the account of the best possible motive, until time and circumstance prove that we were wrong. Where no good motive can be assigned, it may become our duty to suspend our judgment till evidence can be had.

In the application of this rule, it is an undoubted duty to exercise a commendable prudence, by refusing to repose any important trust to the keeping of persons who may be strangers to us, and whose trustworthiness we have never seen tried. But no possible good, but incalculable evil may and does arise from the too common practice of placing all conduct, the source of which we do not fully understand, to the worst of intentions. How often is the gentle, timid soul discouraged, and driven perhaps to despondency, by finding its 'good evil spoken of;' and a well-meant but mistaken action loaded with an evil design!

If the world would but sedulously set about reforming itself on this one point, who can calculate the change it would produce–the evil it would annihilate, and the happiness it would confer! None but an all-seeing eye could at once embrace so vast a result. A result, how desirable! and one that can be brought about only by the most simple process–that of every individual seeing to it that he commit not this sin himself. For why should we allow in ourselves, the very fault we most dislike, when committed against us? Shall we not at least aim at consistency?

Had she possessed less generous self-sacrifice, more knowledge of the world and of business matters in general, and had she failed to take it for granted that others were like herself, and would, when her turn came to need, do as she had done, and find it 'more blessed to give than to receive,' she might have laid by something for the future. For few, perhaps, have ever possessed the power and inclination, in the same degree, at one and the same time, to labor as she has done, both day and night, for so long a period of time. And had these energies been well-directed, and the proceeds well husbanded, since she has been her own mistress, they would have given her an independence during her natural life. But her constitutional biases, and her early training, or rather want of training, prevented this result; and it is too late now to remedy the great mistake. Shall she then be left to want? Who will not answer. 'No!'

HER LAST INTERVIEW WITH HER MASTER

In the spring of 1849, Sojourner made a visit to her eldest daughter, Diana, who has ever suffered from ill health, and remained with Mr. Dumont, Isabella's humane master. She found him still living, though advanced in age, and reduced in property, (as he had been for a number of years,) but greatly enlightened on the subject of slavery. He said he could then see that 'slavery was the wickedest thing in the world, the greatest curse the earth had ever felt–that it was then very clear to his mind that it was so, though, while he was a slave-holder himself, he did not see it so, and thought it was as right as holding any other property.' Sojourner remarked to him, that it might be the same with those who are now slaveholders. 'O, no,' replied he, with warmth, 'it cannot be. For, now, the sin of slavery is so clearly written out, and so much talked against,–(why, the whole world cries out against it!)–that if any one says he don't know, and has not heard, he must, I think, be a liar. In my slaveholding days, there were few that spoke against it, and these few made little impression on any one. Had it been as it is now, think you I could have held slaves? No! I should not have dared to do it, but should have emancipated every one of them. Now, it is very different; all may hear if they will.' Yes, reader, if any one feels that the tocsin of alarm, or the anti-slavery trump, must sound a louder note before they can hear it, one would think they must be very hard of hearing,–yea, that they belong to that class, of whom it may be truly said, 'they have sped their ears that they may not hear.'

She received a letter from her daughter Diana, dated Hyde Park, December 19, 1849, which informed her that Mr. Dumont had 'gone West' with some of his sons–that he had taken along with him, probably through mistake, the few articles of furniture she had left with him. 'Never mind,' says Sojourner, 'what we give to the poor, we lend to the Lord.' She thanked the Lord with fervor, that she had lived to hear her master say such blessed things! She recalled the lectures he used to give his slaves, on speaking the truth and being honest, and laughing, she says he taught us not to lie and steal, when he was stealing all the time himself, and did not know it! Oh! how sweet to my mind was this confession! And what a confession for a master to make to a slave! A slaveholding master turned to a brother! Poor old man, may the Lord bless him, and all slave-holders partake of his spirit!

Also from Benediction Books ...
Wandering Between Two Worlds: Essays on Faith and Art
Anita Mathias
Benediction Books, 2007
152 pages
ISBN: 0955373700

Available from www.amazon.com, www.amazon.co.uk

In these wide-ranging lyrical essays, Anita Mathias writes, in lush, lovely prose, of her naughty Catholic childhood in Jamshedpur, India; her large, eccentric family in Mangalore, a sea-coast town converted by the Portuguese in the sixteenth century; her rebellion and atheism as a teenager in her Himalayan boarding school, run by German missionary nuns, St. Mary's Convent, Nainital; and her abrupt religious conversion after which she entered Mother Teresa's convent in Calcutta as a novice. Later rich, elegant essays explore the dualities of her life as a writer, mother, and Christian in the United States-- Domesticity and Art, Writing and Prayer, and the experience of being "an alien and stranger" as an immigrant in America, sensing the need for roots.

About the Author

Anita Mathias was born in India, has a B.A. and M.A. in English from Somerville College, Oxford University and an M.A. in Creative Writing from the Ohio State University. Her essays have been published in The Washington Post, The London Magazine, The Virginia Quarterly Review, Commonweal, Notre Dame Magazine, America, The Christian Century, Religion Online, The Southwest Review, Contemporary Literary Criticism, New Letters, The Journal, and two of HarperSanFrancisco's The Best Spiritual Writing anthologies. Her non-fiction has won fellowships from The National Endowment for the Arts; The Minnesota State Arts Board; The Jerome Foundation, The Vermont Studio Center; The Virginia Centre for the Creative Arts, and the First Prize for the Best General Interest Article from the Catholic Press Association of the United States and Canada. Anita has taught Creative Writing at the College of William and Mary, and now lives and writes in Oxford, England.

www.anitamathias.com,
christiancogitations.blogspot.com
wanderingbetweentwoworlds.blogspot.com

www.ingramcontent.com/pod-product-compliance
Lightning Source LLC
Chambersburg PA
CBHW020040040426
42331CB00030B/111